Boom Ahoy!

Speculations on Drivers, Timing & Strategy of Booms

Rupert M Hart

Published by CordaNobeloMedia
Version 2.0 Feb 11 2013 (ver 46)
Version 3.0 Feb 11 2013 (ver 49)
Version 4.0 Mar 4 2013 (ver 54)

Library of Congress Cataloging-in-Publication Data: for ordering information see back cover.

Acknowledgements

Special thanks to: Marie, Max and Torsten.

What People Say about Rupert Hart's books

"Recession Storming: Thriving in Downturnws through Superior Marketing, Pricing and Product Stategies," 2008.

"This is a great business book and immensely timely. I recommend it highly. It's full of actionable ideas that marketing and business development people, as well as business owners, can use today." Bob Pettigrew, Chairman, Worldwide Consulting Company.

"As a Harvard MBA with several start-ups under my belt in good times and bad, I found this book quite refreshing. While most business books take 200 pages [...] this one contains kernels of wisdom in nearly each paragraph, and packs a wallop in a short, tight read." Arthur Zwern, Serial Entrepreneur.

"I loved this book! Rupert Hart's book "Recession Storming" is chock-full of practical, insightful and resourceful tips for helping your company thrive during an economic or sector-based downturn. Hart's book is easy to read with a massive amount of real-world examples. It is well organized with a very detailed table of contents and index. In addition, each chapter is well structured with the concept, the supporting sections, and the summarizing conclusion. I highly recommend this book to anyone who wants to help their company not just survive but thrive." David Richer, Division Manager, Software Technology Company

"As the owner of a real estate franchise and a financial advisory firm, I am in markets down 40% on last year, so I understand first hand just what being in a recession is like. Rupert Hart is right when he says it is more like feeling becalmed than being in a storm. In those circumstances, it's all to easy to hunker down, succumb to torpor and hope things will get better. I know. For business owners and managers who realize that to survive and thrive in a recession, you actually need to TAKE ACTION, Rupert Hart's book will appeal because it is packed full of ideas to improve revenues from existing clients and to price intelligently to raise margins. I went through the book systematically making checklists of Rupert Hart's ideas that I can implement in my 2 businesses. The long "To Do" lists I made testify to its usefulness. Now I'm moving into execution mode." "Business Owner" (Coventry, UK)

"Recession Storming is an insightful and entertaining look at the inevitability of business cycles and the opportunities unique to [...] recession. As a corporate president in the health care industry, I found Mr. Hart's book to be an accurate analysis of business principles, made accessible to the lay reader. During this time of political fear mongering, Recession Storming is an optimistic reminder that all is not lost and indeed for the courageous and well-informed, advantages exist. Seize the day, and this book!." Vance Landis, Healthcare CEO.

"As an MBA and independent marketing consultant, I found this book to be chock full of great ideas that I can immediately suggest to several of my clients." Emma Zolbrod MBA, Independent Marketing Consultant.

CrowdFunding Your Startup! Raising Venture Capital using New CrowdFunding Techniques, 2012.

"With pragmatic wisdom, brutal honesty and a dose of wicked vulgarity, Rupert Hart takes the budding entrepreneur through the challenges of getting a startup funded. If you think that crowdfunding is easy - then think again - this book will teach you to approach your funders professionally. It will give you insights into how venture investors think."

"What I like about Rupert Hart is his writing style. Unlike so many authors who write dry and hard to digest financial guidance books, Mr. Hart's prose makes you want to keep reading."

"One of the first accessible resources for those interested in crowdfunding. The prose is very accessible with engaging examples to support the major points."

"The book has every thing you need to know legally, a great resource list at the back, and includes the actual Jobs Act."

*"I found Rupert Hart's latest book extremely informative and helpful.
This book was well written, concise and easy to follow."*

"This book is very well researched and the concepts are clearly described. It is also extremely timely. I highly recommend this excellent book."

Contents

About the Author

Rupert Hart is the author of "Recession Storming," a well-known book on recession strategy which was number one on Amazon.com on books on recession for 4 years. It was published in March 2008, 9 months before it was announced we were in recession. He originally wrote that book and published it in 1992. He has been thinking about business cycles and contrarian thinking for several decades. Realizing that a recession is often the train wreck of a boom gave him insights to write this book on booms.

The name "Rupert Hart" is not a pseudonym; it's my real name. People laugh at forecasters who get it wrong. But they shouldn't, for three reasons. First, this is a book about analysis of mechanisms and speculations of possibilities, and there is no shame in a thought experiment. Second, the world is full of wimps, and doesn't need another. A forecast is still useful even if it is not accurate. Let's get over it. Third, by posing a thought experiment and looking for clues or green lights, we can together develop an insight which you can profit from. That's worth doing.

He has been an operating manager, management consultant, venture capitalist and business owner. He holds an MBA from INSEAD, the leading European Business School. He is married and lives near Silicon Valley, California.

Why you should read this book

I know I am going to be wrong,
You know I am going to be wrong,
I know you know that I am going to be wrong.

Any book about the next boom must be wrong. This book, too.

The future is unknowable. All we have is the past to derive insights from, a little knowledge of what is already happening in the murky recesses of the economy, and a few speculations to project forward with. I believe even these simple speculations will be helpful, even if wrong. My aim is to help you gauge the arrival of a boom in advance for yourself.

Why you should listen to me

Many years ago I wrote a book on recession strategy and later began to perceive there was a gap on books about boom strategy. I asked my friends about what should be in it. "Just write it as if someone was reading your recession book backwards" is what my friend said. Aha! An intriguing thought because recessions often follow booms and are caused by the excesses that cause the boom. By chance I had become like an airplane accident investigator hired as a consultant by aircraft manufacturers! But it turned out a boom is rather more than that.

Why you should care about a Boom

There are several reasons this should be a subject of great interest to you:

This is a defining moment for your career.

Most people will only have one or two booms in their careers, and this one will be the defining moment of your career. This is the boom where you pay off the house, build wealth and ensure your legacy. Can you afford to miss out?

You can change your future.

Why should you care about what is or is not going to happen in a few years anyway? It is not in your power to make it happen, and you will enjoy the moment when it comes anyway. So why should you give it any thought, since you already have plenty to keep you busy now, thank you very much?

You don't want to miss out.

Now you are probably asking yourself why you should really worry about what might happen in 5 years time. After all, you have enough to worry about now. And why worry about good things coming towards you. Especially if you can't influence events, anyway. Well, they say that a rising tide lifts all boats, and that is true, but it can also lift some more than others. Maybe even some that couldn't not have floated at all without a high tide. Think of it this way. Imagine you are walking all the road after a boom has passed and perhaps you are worried about meeting your house payments Along the street comes your high school buddy, which happens to be driving a nice new Mercedes he acquired in the boom, and offers you a ride. How are you going to feel? That's why I urge you to take on board some of the things I am going to say, so that you don't get left behind.

Wealth is made by thinking ahead.

If you have the moxie for it, the ones who think differently are the ones who can really clean up. How many people saw a recession and a stock market crash coming in 2007? Not many. Even the Queen of England asked why no one saw it coming (considering she paid them real money to give her advice). Well, John Paulson became a rather legendary investor for betting on what would happen and made a billion on the housing crisis. We didn't, he did. He was willing to be a contrarian and was prepared for a rare opportunity.

A little information goes a long way

As a boy, my father and I would go sailing and he would ask me to brace myself and haul in sail, saying there was a fair breeze coming on 5 seconds time. I asked him how Ion earth he knew. As those of you who are sailors know, it was because he could see the signs in the change on color of the water due to small ripples caused by the wind in the near distance ("wind lines") and coming towards us. Sometimes a little knowledge can be very useful, eh?

You need to escape groupthink.
Speculations, or thought experiments, can be a counterpoint to the "groupthink" where everybody thinks the same thing and it is difficult to see other view points. Remember when the dot.com craze was at its highest? Jim Valentine, legendary venture capitalist, apologized and said "we all drank the same Kool-Aid." Even if you don't agree with everything I say, maybe I can help you see things differently and guide you to some useful techniques you can adopt and modify for yourself. That is my hope.

Why there is a boom coming.
There are three reasons to be cheerful about why a boom is coming.

The first is that economies do not stay in recession or a trough for ever. This is a mixture of human behavior and changes around the world bringing growth that jumpstarts growth for all. Most recessions last only 11-13 months.

The second is that it is exceedingly rare for recoveries to remain slow quiet and gradual. They almost all lead to explosive growth which is the boom.

The third is that there has almost never been a period when a boom did not appear within 10 years of the last boom

Structure of this book
After introducing a boom in a general way, we split the task of speculating on the boom into three parts. Part 1: Boom Timing investigates what are the impediments and hindrances to a

boom, how long a recovery takes, and what have been typical timings in the past. Part 2: Boom Drivers looks at what are the conditions for starting a boom, how to spot when a boom is about to occur, and what drives it forward. Part 3: Boom Strategy helps suggest strategies for taking advantage of a boom, preparing beforehand, and allowing for a recession at the end. Let's start with the timing of a boom.

A boom is the Daddy of growth and the culmination of all that growth since the last recession. Most of the opportunities in the business cycle lie in this fantastic two year period. I am sure you are feeling that after a deep financial crisis which has left the world in a daze, that a boom seems unlikely so let's address those concerns now. Don't miss it!

Introduction: What is a boom?

Booms don't appear out of nowhere, suddenly and fully formed. They are nurtured silently, they feed on certain economic conditions, and take time to build and spread.

So what is a boom, exactly?
Here's how to define what a boom is. Take a look at the business cycle. After a recession, there is a period of recovery. When the economy has caught up to where it was before the recession, this period of growth is called a recovery. This goes on for several years and then a self-reinforcement goes on that massively accelerates growth. I call this the boom. This period usually lasts 1-2 years. That is all. Then the boom ends in a recession.

Wikipedia's explanation of a boom is: *A period that follows recovery phase in a standard economic cycle. A boom is characterized by an economy working at full or near-full capacity, strong consumer demand, low rate of unemployment, and a rising stock market, usually accompanied by rapidly increasing consumer prices (inflation).*

A boom is actually what most of US think about when we think of business and life. The happy times. The "fun bit." Barbequing by the lake, buying garden furniture, going on exotic vacations, putting money in the stock market, smiling. The bad news is that booms end in recessions, and booms are really only about a quarter of our lives. The rest is misery and slow growth. Interestingly, there are few or no books about how to take advantage of such a special time as a boom, which is what this book is for: to fill that gap.

What's the difference between a bubble, fad, trend and a boom?
It is worth trying to define the difference between booms bubbles, fads and trends. There are several books out there

that are wonderful about explaining all the major trends out there. Trends in demographics, wealth and health, technology and population. Wonderful stuff. Most entertaining to read and to dream about. But, while it seems even glaciers have developed legs recently, they may influence the upcoming boom, but over such a short period, we have to be careful not to assign importance to trends which cannot but tangentially influence a boom. Here's what Wikipedia says about fads, trends and bubbles:

A fad is any form of behavior that develops among a large population and is collectively followed with enthusiasm for some period, generally as a result of the behavior's being perceived as novel in some way. A fad is said to "catch on" when the number of people adopting it begins to increase rapidly. The behavior will normally fade quickly once the perception of novelty is gone.

Trend: Though the term trend may be used interchangeably with fad, a fad is generally considered a fleeting behavior whereas a trend is considered to be a behavior that evolves into a relatively permanent change.

Bubble: An economic bubble (sometimes referred to as a speculative bubble, a market bubble, a price bubble, a financial bubble, a speculative mania or a balloon) is "trade in high volumes at prices that are considerably at variance with intrinsic values." It could also be described as a trade in products or assets with inflated values.

Individual companies act like minibooms. Enron, Madoff, WorldCom, etc were beset by fraud. But not before they announced they had invented new business models. In these cases their performance was not factual.

Many years ago I wrote a book on recessions, and having read about and personally experienced quite a few recessions, it is almost a joke how often the phrase "this time it's different" comes up. Often almost exactly that phrase, too! Of course, some things are different,. But what they really ,means is" no, this is not a bubble or passing fad, but a real trend that is here to stay". Well, maybe. Maybe not. Don't forget that a boom is not here to stay so some of the things they talk about in a boom are also doomed. They are bubbles or fads. I suppose the difference between bubbles and fads is the presence of money, which expands any passing fad into an inflated bubble.

What it's like to be in a boom?

I was there at the Dotcom peak in San Francisco and Silicon Valley, at the start of 2000. For many of US that was the height of a boom and how we define it. Let me remind you what it was like.

Every night you seemed to get several invites for companies doing their launch parties of parties to meet potential recruits or friends or to bring their friends. San Francisco had more restaurants per capita than any other city on the planet, as the parties were fuelled by venture capital money. Everybody was young, ostentatious, wanting to get rich and change the world. Money was spent like water.

During the day, everywhere where food or drink or coffee was sold were people meeting, who would be hatching plans of another startup. In hush-hush tones, of course, lest someone steal the next big thing.

Companies spent lavishly on rebuilding premises with the theory of building credibility and attracting new people. Wild colors, even a board table held up by hot air (boo.com).

There was no limit to inexperience. I once met a friend who said he was due to launch his internet company in 28 countries and had only one day to open up France the next day.

People seemed to work crazy hours, and across time zones. It seemed no one ever met anyone in the same company except at "all hands" meetings: even neighboring cube-mates would swap emails in quietness. Business development became the new name for sales. Nobody ever seem to take their vacations in case they missed out.

Babies were delayed and so dating on match.com became an interview session as women in their early forties struggled to find someone in the next few years to have a baby with. There were so many IVF operations producing twins that San Carlos had its own Twins Club (I know one of the Presidents).

Releasing Human Desires
"Money allows you to be who you truly are" George Clooney character in the movie "Ocean's Eleven." Economists love to think of human beings as rational beings only interested in increasing their net worth. But you and I know that we have desires and we are human. When we have the money we can spend it where we like. And we do. And consumers are a very important factor in most economies.

Let's look at those human desires for clues as to where money flows in a boom.

*In contrast with recessions, t*he desire to be free is a powerful force, perhaps the most powerful there is. In a recession many people live in fear and do not feel free at all. In a boom, people are released from fear because they can now meet their needs and can now allow free rein to their desires. It is not as if their human desires change, only during a recession, many of theme are suppressed. This release is a tremendous thing.

Massive change in spending patterns. A recession is a time when many people and companies have no cash to buy anything that isn't absolutely critical. A boom is quite the opposite. It's important to realize the amazing difference between the two, when your mind may be stuck in the mire of a recession or slow recovery.

In a recession, for example, people are often unable to buy a product that might save them some money if they do not have the money to invest in it. For example, a contractor might want to buy a new chop saw that is more efficient and makes better cuts than his existing one but doesn't have the cash, even if the payback period is very short. Or, a consumer wants to buy a solar panel which would save him money but cannot front the cash. In these environments, pricing trade-offs are quite different from booms, where financing is assumed to be easily available and the customer can easily work out his payback.

Let's look at disposable income. If we can understand that, then we can understand the way consumers, investors, service-providers and governments spend. Let's start with a recession. In a recession, it is usually a struggle to pay for even the basics. Individuals eat ramen noodles, don't go out for dinner much, take "staycations" rather than vacations, and sell assets to pay for their spending. Their sources of cash like credit cards and second mortgages are massively curtailed and they start to pay off debt. They have very little disposable or discretionary income. Every cent that comes in goes straight out.

In a boom everything is different. Imagine your assets increase in value another 20%. Imagine you earn just 10% more than you spend. Imagine your credit cards are somewhat paid off and the limits are increased. You feel more secure in your job. You now have disposable income, the credit capacity and the confidence to use it. For suppliers of frivolous products, this is a time of plenty after the desert.

Your friends are having fun and you want to be part of it. You know people who are making more money more easily by investing and you want your money to multiply so you invest with them. You can spare the cash, so you do. Even spending on boats is seen as investment. And when you are working hard earning money, you feel you deserve a reward, seeing it as an investment in yourself.

Booms are times when greatness shows. Rembrandt could not have brought his wonderful art to the fore at any other time than a boom because he would not have been able to make a living painting portraits, except when the rich patrons wanted to immortalize themselves after they had made a great deal of money from the boom in spices in Holland in the 1770a.

Increase in Competition

It might seem nonsensical that competition might increase in a boom. After all, after a recession where demand is severely constrained yet there are still the same players, competition might be expected to be fierce. So how can a boom engender increased competition?

Let's try an analogy from the Natural world. In a desert you would expect that there would be few snakes because there is very little for them to prey on. And that is the case, with one snake every few square miles. In a humid jungle, however, there will be many animals and plants and therefore you would expect lots of snakes. In a documentary I once saw about a film crew in Papua New Guinea's rainforest, the camera crew had to endure one poisonous snake almost every meter up a path. In other words, there are more competitors when there is more for the to feed off. Supply of snakes increases as supply of prey increases. The exact ratio of prey per snake may tip either way from one situation to another but where information on location of prey is easily available and snakes are very mobile. You could expect to see several snakes fight it out for a piece of the prey, whereas in a desert it is perhaps possible for two snakes in one area not to meet.

In a lush environment, we expect many different varieties, all trying to exploit niches. In a desert we would expect different mutations. Therefore the competition will not only be more common but different.

In a recession, prices come under pressure as competitors try hard to get sales. There are fewer contracts or product sales at that time, and more competitors will come into the market from adjacent areas. So, yes, competition will be hard-nosed.

In a recovery and a boom, demand increases and many niches open up as customers exert their preferences and competition moves away from price to other features. New players enter markets, especially service companies and startups. Everybody is trying to gain price premium and/or increase sales; marketing expenditures go through the roof as they try to differentiate themselves and sell their "story". With plenty of profit to go around, you would think that everyone would get fat and happy and not begrudge other companies their revenues. But everybody in the chain of profit-pool-dippers will get greedy and more demanding.

In the end, therefore, booms produce a different but more intense competition.

A few thoughts to start with

1. Everybody wants a boom It is in everyone's interest to stoke the fires of a boom. Everybody really wants those happy times. This means even the faintest sparks of a boom are fanned into a conflagration by the combined puff of everybody. The desire for a boom is pent-up and overpowering.

2. Timeframe is less than 10 years. There's never been a period in US history when there hasn't been a boom within 10 years of a recession. So, it is pointless to contemplate any developments that aren't very likely to be important in the next five or so years. This is not what you normally hear, is it! Ten years is a short time, and the boom is likely to arrive even earlier than that, see below.

3. Booms only really last a brief 2 years

All the action is in the last 2 years of the growth recovery. It's all over too quickly and it ends abruptly. If you like, the Boom is the orgasm of the recovery. Without the boom, the recovery would be nothing. (Maybe that is why sex is called "Boom Boom" in South America? Or Bunga Bunga in Italy!)

This means that any long plans beyond the boom period will be launching into the vacuum of a recession and will be wasted. This is a very important point that many people neglect to notice. They are the ones who are massively overextended when a recession hits and they keep dancing while the music plays even if the music volume starts to wind down. Plan carefully!

Two years is a remarkably short time. Just 730 days, 8 seasons, 2 summers. A lot happens in a very short period. It is all over too quickly. Most of us find ourselves saying "wow, I was just getting started". Don't be in that position!

4. The Fed wants a boom
The Federal Reserve Bank may be nominally independent of the government but they like to be liked and they respond to their charter to keep steady growth without much inflation and unemployment. Since the 1990s they err on the side of booms rather than busts, so you can be sure they will try hard to keep conditions beneficial for a boom.

5. Booms are robust creatures
It takes a lot to steer a boom off course. Even Sept 11 2001 caused only a minor story and drop in output. A boom is going to happen and you can take advantage of it. It is in everyone's interest so there are very powerful forces driving it forward. Have faith.

6. Fairly regular Having said that, we cannot rely on a predictability of timing. Economists dislike the phrase of business cycle because it implies that there is regular timing in the ups and downs of the economy. It is true there is considerable variation in the timings, and so they call them economic fluctuations. However there do seem to be minimum and maximum limits on boom timings, from which we can learn. Also, booms do seem to happen sometime: there never has been a period without a boom, so it is important to look ahead a few steps.

7. We can still predict even if we do not understand the causes. How many people would be willing to bet against the rising of the Sun tomorrow? The Ancients built buildings to predict many movement of the stars in the sky; we do not even now understand the cause of gravity, yet we can still base our plans on the likely appearance of the Sun. In the same way, we can use what information we have to look ahead. Hell, economists are still arguing over the causes of the Great Depression almost a century after!

8. Growth is important for all of us, and a boom even more important!

Some people see growth as a growth in material possessions which causes pollution and therefore they are against it. But growth is important for all of us because it allows for new opportunities. Imagine if the job market never grew and there would be very little movement between companies and you would wait for ever for an opening to appear. Imagine if everybody was quite happy with the way they have always done things and you would never be able to get anyone's time to listen to your pitch about a new product or service. Growth therefore is important for all us.

Part 1: Boom Timing

Chapter 1.1: Theories of Boom Timing

Everybody wants to know when the next boom is coming. There are many theories about boom timing:

- Business Cycle
- Time to Recover
- Political Cycle
- Trends since the Second World War
- This Time it's Different, Really!

Business Cycle Theory

Looked at from afar, it would seem that booms and recessions are short and inconsequential blips on the seemingly-ever-upward progress of the GDP. If you look at a chart of GDP growth over a century, you have to look hard to see those fluctuations. Over a decade those fluctuations matter, and over a few years they really matter. For the above-trend areas are the booms, and the below-trend areas the recessions.

It is obvious that there are economic fluctuations and that, quarter to quarter, GDP grows at varying rates. If you chart changes in GDP against time, the business cycle theory takes shape as a steady growth over several years, a very fast growth through several more, a very rapid decline over a year, a slow growth over several years, a regular expansion and then a sharp drop again. It certainly does seem that the economy cycles up and down; hence business cycle.

It might not seem much to see a 6% fall in GDP in a year, as in a recession, since that implies 94% is doing quite nicely. But it turns out that that 6% drop is not across the board but rather in certain areas which are massively affected with 40% or 100% falls. It's easy to overlook booms in the same way.

The business cycle theory is that recessions are always followed by recovery, expansion and then boom which is then followed by recession. There are many likely explanations of this cycle using "animal spirits" euphoria, herd behavior, diminishing returns to investment. It must be a fairly good explanation of boom timing because booms do often appear with a strange regularity and can often be foreseen in advance by outside observers.

The first is that, booms seem to occur about every 6-10 years, an average of 8 years (technically 7.8 years) since World War 2. The last boom was nominally 2007 so that would make 2007+8=2015. If we factor in the 6-10 range, then you could reasonably assume that the boom would occur in 2007+6=2013 to 2007+10=2017. So, theory 1 gives 2013 to 2017, with an average of 2015.

Time Needed to Recover

Now, not all booms and recessions are alike. As shown in Carmen Reinhart and Ken Rogoff's book, recessions after a banking crisis take rather longer than normal and so we would expect a boom to be delayed. And you could well argue that a deeper-than-normal recession like the "Great Recession" of 2007-2009 would leave a slower recovery. On a hunch, let's add a year or two to these above figures. So we get 2014 to 2018, and so maybe 2016 seems reasonable.

Political Cycle.

Turns out, that there is a noticeable correlation between booms in the economy and elections. Funny that! Not entirely causal, you understand, just a remarkable coincidence. At the beginning of a President's term of office he or she will naturally appear prudent, cutting where necessary and putting the house in order, blaming the previous incumbent as needed. Then they will attempt to engineer a re-election by strengthening the economy and getting full employment where possible, and making sure inflation is in control. ("It's the Economy, Stupid" and all that!). That leads to a rather handy boom just in election year. (However the Economy is rarely so easily tricked and it is often that a recession follows right after an election, even if the same person is elected). In 2016, we will have another Presidential election. So that would lead to a boom in 2016, possibly 2015.

Research shows that it is growing unemployment not the absolute level of unemployment that worries voters. And other research shows that inflation outguns unemployment in importance for voters, which implies that the Fed may take action to counter inflation and prick nascent bubbles.

Of course not everybody agrees with me. Jim Reid of Deutsche Bank argued in his Long Term Asset Study that, if you take the average recovery period of the last 33 cycles since 1854, that the next recession is due in 2012. My belief, however, is that conditions and the ability to extend recoveries has been better managed (you might disagree) since the Second World War. Applying his argument to the last 2 recovery periods would lead to much shorter expansions than actually happened, so somewhat killing his own argument. [1]

Trends since the Second World War
Many people argue, not unreasonably, that the period of prosperity after the War means we have to modify our understanding of boom timing.

This Time it's different, really!
You could argue that these economic fluctuations are small and not very unpredictable. And you might be right. But I suggest that the enormous growth we are seeing from China and India growth could be like a tsunami against these ripples: it could overwhelm them in intensity. All to the good of the boom theory.

Therefore, if we put all these three theories together, I am willing to hang out my shingle on 2015-2016 as the years of the next boom.

Chapter 1.2: Getting there from here

Agreed: the world faces large challenges. But I still believe we will have a boom, and shortly. Why do I think that? Well, I don't think we need to solve all these problems for there to be a boom. Problems can be solved, yes, but they can also be deferred, swept under the rug, defused or worked around. (We are good at that in the US.) My aim here is not to say that there are no problems, but there is a reasonable chance that we can get around these obstacles to enable a boom to happen.

And you would be surprised how often the same aspects of booms pop up every cycle: it seems there is a distinct loss of memory going on. You think collateralized mortgage obligations (or, CMOs) were a concept of the last recession and boom? Wrong! I happened to pick up Michael Lewis' book, "Liar's Poker," published in 1990 and which covered the boom of 1987. Guess what? CMOs figured strongly then, too, fully 2 booms before the next one.

What would really kill a boom?
Booms, once growing, are hard to kill. But they are not immortal, and they will certainly end in a few years as the natural order of things. But it is worth our while to consider what would stop it dead in its tracks.

The first thing that came to mind was war. But wait, we are already involved in several of them, though mostly against non-national enemies. So perhaps a major war including China (Taiwan?, a trade spat?), a nuclear war, or a major terrorist incident on US soil (dirty bomb in New York?), or a deliberate act of aggression by a foreign state.

A major natural disaster might do it. But then again, Hurricane Katrina devastated New Orleans., the BP Macondo oil spill in the Gulf of Mexico, Japan's Fukushima nuclear accident have caused but hiccups. Perhaps it would take a big problem in a major US City, maybe a California Earthquake, or a tsunami affecting New York.

State and govt debt, deficits & Liabilities
Since the US has been running a budget deficit for some time (i.e. We are spending more than we are earning), the US is vulnerable to foreigners not buying Treasury bonds to finance this deficit. If they felt that the US is in danger of defaulting because it is spending beyond its means, they may stay away from US bond sales or demand much higher interest rates to compensate for the risk. Higher interest rates would choke off a growing economy and diminish spending power for those heavily in debt. A reduction in interest in bond auctions would force the government to enact higher spending cuts than expected. All of these changes would reduce the growth of the economy.

Therefore Congress will be forced eventually to cut spending and increase taxes. If there is extensive wrangling, then financial markets may lose confidence. If however, real cuts are implemented, then the economy may be heavily impacted. My guess is that a middle road will be found, with most of the costs and tax increases being deferred until after the 2016 election.

The other aspect to realize is that the US does own significant assets which it could sell. Imagine visiting your grandma for a coffee. She complains she can't afford milk. You look around and remind her that she lives in a house worth $500k. In the same way that everyone says the US is broke they ignore the tremendous assets the US has that can be released.

The Dollar. And what of the Dollar? For decades the trade figures show the US has been importing more than it is exports. In order to fund this, the US has been selling dollars in the form of treasury bonds and currency which is held by foreigners. Currency analysts worry that demand for this will dry up and worry that the dollar will drop precipitously. Yet it hasn't dropped much. Several reasons come to mind. Many of those imports are in fact imports for US corporations' subsidiaries abroad, others are imports that are incorporated into products of US corporations and some re-exported. Also, the US, with its strong laws and stable economy is considered a safe haven. However, my guess is that the dollar will decline slowly. This makes it easier for foreigners to buy our products, but harder for US to import products.

Retirement What was special about 2011? 2011 was a landmark year: the year the first Baby boomers retired. After the Second World War, the GIs came back and celebrated as we all would. Their children, born from 1946, have now reached the age of retirement of 65 (1946+65=2011). Yes, yes, Demographics. Usually when we think demographics (and let's face it we have all read books about demographics as of the last 30 years) we think of a slow moving glacier, that moves so slowly as not be noticeable for ages. Well, the glacier has developed legs and is now beginning to move fast at last. And as the saying goes "demographics is destiny" because we can see it happening beforehand. The number of 85 years old is due to triple in a just a few years, and the average age of the country (currently 38) is growing old fast.

Why does this matter? Two reasons: unfunded Medicare/ Medicaid and Social Security, and what they do with their investment funds.

Oil Price

Oil is a major cost for all countries because we all use so much of it. If the oil price goes up too much too quickly, then demand destruction occurs: we find ways to drive less, and use less energy. It uses up money we could use on other things and therefore squeezes revenue for other companies.

Several effects drive up the oil price.

a. Increased demand for oil. In a boom, especially with the Asian boom and their manufacturing for their infrastructure and for the Developed World, there will be a massive increase in demand. I a boom, that demand can increase very very quickly. So fast that supply cannot pick up fast enough. This explains the spike in oil price in 2008 to $147.

b. Inadequate supply of oil. Most of the world's oil is supplied by OPEC and so they if they find that demand is high they can increase supply. However they are inefficient economies and they need a high price to pay for their economies. They may also choose to increase the price to slow down the use of the oil, increasing the value of the oil in the ground.

c. Threats of disruption to oil supply

d. Peak Oil fears.

e. Availability of substitutes.

f. Speculation and hot money

In my mind, it is in most people's interests to not increase the oil price too quickly.

Foreign turmoil. As Fareed Zakaria pointed out in his book "The Post-American Future," it is remarkable that the stock market and the GDP often ride merrily along with nary a backward glance at news headlines. This might seem incredible. But think back to what you know about the '50s and '60s. You're probably thinking it was a time of steady prosperity and increasing standard of living. And it was. But the headlines screamed Cold War, Korean War and Cuban Missile Crisis. (Of course, to be fair, this was a time when the Government was massively stimulating the economy by spending on the Military-Industrial Complex, so perhaps Zakaria's argument is weak today). Perhaps, in our more-interconnected world, that will be less of the case, but still worth thinking about. Especially if there is oil involved.

Housing. At the peak, some 30% of the houses ion the US were under foreclosure or underwater. This would seem a crippling holdup on the road to the boom. People cannot easily move to where they can find a job, and their wealth is seriously constrained. In addition some 10 million mortgages will "reset" to a higher interest rate in 2013. But we have seen this problem before and will see it again. Growth in the economy will work most of the problem out and when asset prices rise, the house market will stabilize and start to appreciate. This is a problem that will go away with time. Most commentators believe the foreclosure peak will have been in 2012.

Unemployment. At its peak, unemployment stood at about 9% with some underemployment totaling about 20%, with some potential workers intimidated from re-entering the workforce and looking for a job because it seems jobs are scarce and seeking is hard work. In recoveries, employers tend to take time to hire back workers. They wait to see definite signs of recovery, they increase the productivity of the existing workers, they offer overtime, until they cannot resist hiring again. Growth will solve this one, too.

Flation=Inflation or Deflation
In a recession, the Fed is very concerned with deflation: this is where prices go down and customers withhold their spending because they think prices will be cheaper shortly. Deflation is a very exceptional event, in general, but Japan has had 2 decades of it, prices have been under pressure due to the Internet and China price, so this is a concern. My guess is that deflation worries will go away and inflation will be the biggest issue.

2008 was a recent peak in oil prices and many food prices. Oil rose from about $70 to $142 a barrel. Most commentators say this was due to more rapid demand than expected from the growing countries of Asia with supply unable to keep up. This inflation was a serious determinant in the recession.

Inflation is often considered as either a supply-led inflation or a demand-led inflation. Supply-led inflation is due to an increase in prices due to supply constraints. Demand-led inflation is due to people being richer and using their money to buy things. Milton Friedman, Nobel Prize-winning economist said that "inflation was every where and in every way money led" and so governments try to keep the money supply under control.

The European Central Bank put up interest rate at that time to try to reduce the impact of inflation on its economy. The added costs for many products and services are surely a cause in the last recession. Governments are very wary of letting inflation get out of control. It causes their citizens pain. President Carter was forced to massively increase interest rates to stop inflation from its 16% level and this caused the sharp government-induced recession of 1981-2. Inflation is one of the Federal Reserve's major remits. China's previous Premier Wen Jiabao was heard to explain in 2011 that "inflation is like a tiger: you daren't let it out of its cage." So inflation and the effects of fighting it could diminish a boom.

But I think that it is unlikely that a large bout of inflation will be allowed to happen and governments will try hard to avoid hard landings and will strive for gentle growth.

Climate change. So what of the end of the planet and the effects of climate change? How can I ignore the elephant in the room? How can you lay any store on what I say if I cannot solve that problem, the biggest problem facing humanity since we emerged from the primordial slime and later became a separate species some 100,000 years ago? And what of the world population's growing need for water, for affordable food, for energy? What is my answer, you say? Well, fair point. I will argue that solutions to these problems may make up drivers of the boom, but they are moving too slowly and are not yet powerful enough to stop the immense pressure for a boom. In my talks, people at this point accuse me of being flippant, so I apologize if the bile is rising in your throat. I believe a boom is powerful force of nature on its own. And that is because humans are powerful and desire peace and prosperity more than anything else. Climate, water, energy are not yet powerful enough to arrest that immoveable glacier.

FAQs

What might disturb the timing of a boom? Two things come to mind. The first are external shocks. Or, as a former UK Prime Minister, Harold Macmillan, used to say , "Events, my dear boy, Events!" (you can imagine a Brit saying that, can't you?). The World seems a little more prone than normal to "black swan" events where low probability events seem to have large effects.

As Carmen Reinhart and KenRogoff showed, after a banking crisis recession, like that of 2007-2009, there is a risk of a double dip recession.

Couldn't we have a lost decade like the Japanese Yes, we could, but I don't think we will. The Japanese you remember were the upcoming nation in the late 1980s. Then they had a real estate meltdown and the banks became insolvent. They have spent two decades with zombie banks not lending and the Japanese no longer saving, and a period of time of deflation where people tend not to buy things because they expect the price to go down shortly. This is a disaster for the Japanese people. The real estate market and the stock market have not recovered to the heights of 2 decades ago and now the financial crisis of 2008-9 has given them a very high debt ratio. I don't think this will happen to the US because our debt ratio will remain considerably lower, because our banks have separated their bad assets from good assets (allowing them to lend again) and because the Federal Reserve Bank is taking many actions to avoid deflation. I don't think we need fear deflation.

What if China and Asia overheat

Many countries in Asia have been providing significant growth to US corporations and stimulating the economy. But they have been growing very quickly, at almost 10%. The demands for their economies for commodities and food is causing supply shortfalls and prices are spiking. This inflation may cause unrest as well as wage increases. Typically governments try to slow down economies by increasing interest rates and forcing banks to set aside more capital, so diminishing their funds available. Problem is, this can increase their currency values which increases hot money flowing in, making the problem worse. Recently there seems to be overcapacity but if these estimates are wrong then the economies may reach their limits faster then expected. In which case there will be tremendous spillover effects around the world as demand reduces. There are several forecasts out there that indicate a slowdown of China growth especially from 2015; this might lead to a recession.

What shocks would kill a boom dead.
A boom will always come to an end. Like human beings it will come to a natural end when its excesses contain the roots of its demise, out of sheer old age, or it will die when a shock hits it, like dying in a road accident. Shocks are always a risk. By their nature they are unexpected. It is hard to plan for every shock. But you can be prepared to expect some form of shock.

Fortunately most shocks, even the really big ones, can have a smaller effect that you might imagine. Especially if they occur nearer the beginning of the expansion. Perhaps this is like a tough boisterous healthy teenager falling out of a window at a party and suffering bruises, compared to a brittle octogenarian falling on ice and suffering a hip break.

Take Sept 11 for example. The sudden and shocking tragedy of the Sept 11 2001 World Trade Center terrorist attack definitely caused a recession in 2001 and 2002. Almost 3000 people died in one incident: 10 times more than the next biggest terrorist attack, and as many as were killed in Pearl Harbor in 1941. But it was short-lived and the boom of 2007 happened anyway.

A big war would kill it dead. The world is more interconnected today than ever and uncertainty is enough to cause cardiac arrest. The earthquake and power shortages caused by the tsunami in Fukushima in Japan in 2011 caused massive disruptions to the supply chain of several electronic companies and they were reporting reduced earnings for 6 months afterwards. It is like the stern wave of a boat: if the boat stalls, the stern wave may come over the transom.

Couldn't a rise in interest rates choke off the recovery and delay a boom?
This might be a real risk, especially as European and Japanese governments, as well as emerging countries, increase their interests rates to reduce the impact of inflation. But I think the Fed is well aware of the risks and is deliberately going slowly on increasing interest rates.

Couldn't rising inequality choke the boom?
Many countries' populations are beginning to show a distinct inequality of wealth and income, where a smaller proportion of the population controls a greater than its share of wealth. To some extent this is beneficial, for two reasons: it acts as an incentive for others to earn money, and makes it easier for action to be taken on chasing a opportunity. However, too much inequality can breed resentment as we little people cannot easily have our say. Especially if the richer people are able to avoid their tax obligations. However it can also work the other way, the Galt effect from Ayn Rand's Atlas Shrugged, where the richer ones feel overtaxed and decline to pay excess taxes.

But wasn't the last recession so much deeper than the average recession so won't the boom be delayed much longer?
Possible, but unlikely. Here's why. In the average of recessions are several recessions rather worse than the one we have been through. The recession of 2007-2009 led to unemployment of about 9%, interest rates close to zero, a recession that lasted 13 months, and stock markets and GDP were back to peak levels only 2 years later. The 1980-82 recessions had much lower recovery rates. We could compare to the Depression of 1929-32. There unemployment was 25% at its peak, and the economy was still lower than the peak in 1939, ten years later. This recession was nowhere near that

bad. Therefore a year or two extra should cover the extent of this recession.

It's a thought experiment, of course, so I am allowed to be wrong. But sometimes thought experiments change the way we think. And what if this thought experiment is right? How would you have changed the way you did things over the last boom if you could have gone back in time to 2002? Bet you would have done things differently, wouldn't you? Now consider, that if this thought of 2015-2016 was right, how would you do things differently over the next few years? That is the power of a thought experiment.

Part 2: Boom Drivers

Chapter 2.1: What makes a boom grow

It seems to be a feature of capitalist societies that they experience business cycles of high prosperity and low prosperity. The economy grows steadily and then faster and faster, reaching a peak period of some two years, which is how I define a boom. Then the excesses of that boom suddenly dissipate and a recession follows. Then the economy steadily recovers again, culminating in a boom. And the cycle continues.

Ideally it would be fabulous if we could manage to get continued growth that never leads to a recession. And the Fed is getting better at managing things to get longer period of growth. But the business cycle is not dead.

I am willing to bet that there is a distinct similarity between bunching on a freeway and the causes of recessions. Imagine you are driving. Everybody is going fast and about the same speed. Everyone is keen to get home and perhaps they are all a little close to the car in front. Suddenly a small disturbance occurs. Maybe someone got too close to the car in front and had to brake to avoid a collision. Maybe someone changed lanes suddenly and you have to brake to avoid them. The car behind sees your brake lights and brakes too, because he is a bit close and doesn't have much time or distance to react. If he is going fast and can't figure out how violently you are braking, he may brake hard and slow down fast. The car behind him is also forced to do the same. And soon a ripple of braking spreads backwards down the line of traffic. Eventually someone who has allowed enough distance, or someone who is able to see over the top of the cars in front, brakes gently or slows down and allows more distance so that the ripple subsides. And traffic speeds up. Even if imperfect, analogies like this can be useful ways for figuring out what is about to happen.

The cycle seems to repeat every 6-10 years. This means booms are 6-10 years apart. On average, since the Second World War, they are 7.8 years apart. If we define a boom as

that peak two year period before a recession, then average timings are as follows:
Recession lasting about 11 months
Recovery lasting about 48 months
Boom lasting about 24 months
Followed by recession of about 11 months.

Since booms are the end result of a recovery period and often contain the very cause of a recession, it would be very useful to understand the whole business cycle and what drives it up and down. Let's start with the recovery period after a recession.

Eventually confidence returns and the consumer cannot resist consuming any more. Every dollar they spend is actually multiplied through the economy, which means that small changes become bigger and bigger. In essence a dollar multiplies like rabbits. Here's how. Let's say I buy groceries from you, a mom and pop grocery retailer, for say $20. Let's say you put aside $5 to pay down debt, and spend $15 on vegetables at the market from a farmer. He puts aside $4 and spends $11 on beer at the local bar. The bar spends $6 of this. So here's how the dollar multiplies. Everybody registers the money they receive as their income. So the $20 I spent with you becomes $20 you receive, plus the $15 the farmer received, plus the $11 the bar received. Which equals $46. So $20 dollars becomes $46, or $1 dollar multiples to become $2.3. In this way a small increase in income somewhere trickles down to every corner of the economy.

But wait there's more! Not content with a multiplier, we also have the accelerator to contend with. Here company bosses come to realize there is demand for their products and so they invest in machinery to make more products to take advantage of that opportunity, so as to capture that profit. So they order new equipment. Or, the accelerator is pedal to the metal, you might say. If you are the equipment provider the order comes in and you start your factory going again. Since no one orders in a recession, you may not have had any new orders for several years so this is massively welcome. Now you spend money on people, materials and services to make those bits of machinery and so the money spreads through the multiplier effect.

There's another factor getting things going and that is the inventory question. During a recession, companies reduce the amount they hold of anything and run down their inventories, to conserve cash. But, as the economy picks up in the recovery, they start to realize they are missing out on opportunities to make money as they don't have the physical item the customer wants right now. So they rebuild their inventory, ordering more than are being bought. This helps the growth of the economy.

But there is an extra factor going on here. All this activity stimulates other activity. People talk in bars about how much money they are making, confidence increases and animal spirits are released. There is a tremendous positive feedback effect and all are lifted up. The effect is exponential and you can see a sharply increasing ascent of GDP and activity as the boom begins. In Seth Godin's words, an "ideavirus" spreads contagiously by word of mouth. This leads to a veritable boom effect. Or maybe it is like a tsunami at the moment it approaches the beach; it rises up and accelerates. In fighter aircraft terms, the power to weight ratio is above one and the boom is going vertical.

When I talk to people about booms, the first thing that usually comes to their lips is that they think of a boom as speculative froth or bubbles. Well, booms themselves are short-lived. Only lasting 2 years. Funny thing, though, is that the booms are what we tend to think of a business as usual. But it's not, and we need to recognize this is an exceptional period of time, just 2 years out of 8-10 years. Hey, could be worse. Before the Second World War, you would have spent 40% of your time in recession.

So how do you tell the difference between a recovery after a recession, and a boom? Well, there is no definite dividing line so here are four indicators.

Firstly there is a massive acceleration. A boom is a new peak reached through 2 years of incredible growth. A recovery is a few percent growth per year, a boom is 10% or more, sometimes considerably more. The stock market is a useful indicator as it expresses in figures future expectations of growth better than other factors. The change accelerates as you get closer to the top of the boom, so you can start to feel exponential growth. This is usually seen by insiders as a new ways of doing things, so beware. We have been there before and it is may or not be true, but usually isn't.

Secondly people are engaging in boom-like activities. A boom is a time of excess and therefore we will be engaging in excessive activities. Like drinking from hand painted champagne bottles, like people buying art at fantastic prices, like people being exceedingly arrogant about themselves.

Thirdly indicators are showing trends way above normal trend. I don't mean gross indicators like the stock market, house prices, but key ratios. Such as house price/income ratios, price/earnings ratios, pay for CEOs compared to the lowest-paid worker. It is a fact of history that eventually all ratios revert to the mean. That is, they oscillate about a trend line that is a function of human behavior. Some indicators may change but most do not.

Fourthly, it takes time to build a recovery into a boom. This period is seldom less than 3 years. So, the boom is unlikely to be less than 3-4 years after the last recession.

In these ways you can start to look out for a boom. Of course you should be planning for it sometime before.

Warning: Recession follows Boom
This is the time of "irrational exuberance", only it often seems quite rational to many at the time. At the very peak of the boom, finally all those who have been saying it is only a fad or a bubble finally capitulate and accept that it is a trend into the future.

If the boom is only 5 years after the last peak, then the recession which follows a boom is only 6 years away! So put the date into the calendar and start planning for a recession. Make sure you don't try to time your exit so perfectly you miss it. Make sure, if you can, that your career, company investments and spending will be buttressed against the pains of recession.

How Booms work
A boom is the result of a growth pattern that is started and then becomes self-sustaining and reaches a conflagration. Think of the economic activity as a log of wood in your fireplace. You start it with a match and then it starts to burn. As it burns, the flame heats the wood and more material burns in the air. The fire has become self-sustaining and you don't need to hold the match there any more. The fire heats more of the wood and as the temperature increases so it burins faster. And faster. Until the whole log is fully on fire. So with an economic boom.

What might make the log stop burning is if you withheld the ingredients to make it burn, or douse the fire to cool it below burning temperature. So, if you closed the grate, closed the damper, or took away the wood, or doused the fire with water, or if all the wood was fully used-up, the fire would stop. So with the economy. If the Fed Chairman takes away "the punchbowl" of easy money by increasing interest rates, if an oil shock suddenly makes it expensive to move items around the world or make them, or if a terrorist threat undermines confidence in a stable business environment in which to plan future activities, then the upswing may come to a halt.

Heading into a boom, there are 5 major players involved in making the boom work. We need to look at everyone's behavior and incentives to see why they act the way they do. One of the reasons a boom is so explosive is that it happens to be very beneficial for every party.

The five players are: the consumer, the investor, producers, government (in which I include the Fed), export markets. Another way to see this is consuming, producing, investing, community spending, exporting. Remember always that, since the world is becoming more and more open, the consuming, producing and investing and regulation is not always happening within our shores – there are many more players in the equation than you thought, aren't there? Having read the papers for some time, you will no doubt not be surprised to know that confidence in the future is a critical driver of all expenditures.

The US is an unusual place in that the saying "the consumer is king" is totally true. Some 70% of the economy is due to what a US consumer consumes. In most other countries this is 50% in the UK, going down to 35% in China. Consumers have some basic needs which cannot easily be diminished so consumer spending, especially in the US, is fairly stable. They go out and spend more when they feel confident they will have stable employment, that their incomes are going to increase, that they will not have to face sudden increased expenditures, and when they feel their wealth going up. In addition, the US exports some 6% of its GDP, so foreign consumers are important, too. You could also say that governments are consumers, and producers.

Producers, by which I mean businesses and entities which deliver services and products to consumers, government and regulators.

A boom is wonderfully different from a recession. It's is like migrating to a different ecosystem, one where the climate is much more benign. Imagine walking out of the ice age into

Barbados. You are no longer fighting to survive, but food is plentiful, no effort is required to stay warm, and there is enough of everything that prey leave you alone for the most part.

Like tropical ecosystems, strange creatures emerge blinking into the light. Creatures not seen before. Some are total experiments, but some find a niche and adapt. This is the time of companies with playful names, crazy employee policies, and serving market niches of left-handed tiddlywinks players who speak Papua New Guinean. In a boom, and especially when people of unusual tastes can find what they desire through the Internet, can these ecological niche-dwellers flourish.

Booms are great places for small agile companies, especially in the service sector. Everybody has more disposable income, everybody is willing to experiment a bit, use of time has greater importance, and services are fast to start up. If you were getting wealthy like some of your customers, you would want to use your precious time to make more money or to relax and engage in your fantasizes. As a service provider that's where you can come in.

In a boom, customers seem to be more rational in some way and more factors come into their thinking when choosing a product. In a recession, many customers are so cash-constrained that they are unable to choose a better product, even if it would save them money, of do a better job, if they cannot afford the extra increment of cost. Not so in a boom. Here people make the classic trade-offs between features and cost that we are all taught to think.

In a boom people want to *<u>believe</u>*. They want to believe that growth will continue, that people will be happy and keep spending, and that the boom has become a new level. It is a contagious thought and all are infected.

People seek a story to explain the reason for growth and where to put their efforts. They seek the main driver of the boom, and it is on this that the other drivers of a boom ride. Take the Gold Rush in California in 1849. The story was the discovery of gold that was easy to get out of the ground. Riches for all. The sub story was that the service-providers like classic shovel-sellers made money. Or, the dot com boo of the 1990s where the internet companies attempted to reach stratospheric valuations while the suppliers of routers, switching and communications gear made real profits.

A boom, therefore, rides on the back of a good story. A story of hype and hope. It is your job to figure out what it will be in the future and align yourself with it.

What can we learn from looking at previous booms? There are three different types of booms:

- Focused or localized booms
- General economic booms
- Global booms

Chapter 2.2: Theory of Drivers and SubDrivers

One way to look at the following case-studies of previous booms is that usually there is one powerful story or driver and several drivers that derive from it. Supplying those forces is make generates wealth for the society. The key therefore is align yourself as service-provider, investor and consumer with those drivers.

What makes the difference between recovery and boom and what really makes a boom explode, is a story about hype and hope. It is the time lag between hope and results that fuels the boom!

In the dotcom days, the driver was providing the internet as an information provider. This was the main driver. Communications technology such as internet service providers, routers, optical fiber, cable television all derived from supplying this main driver.

In the 1980s the boom was arguably driven by the deregulation of industry. That was the main driver. A massive financial industry grew to supply the capital to allow companies to consolidate, expand and free themselves from the public sector. This was a subsidiary driver.

2. Many SubDrivers
One of the key messages is that to make something happen, be it a driver or a SubDrivers, you need to have the elements in place, such as technology on the shelf or a large portion of the populace ready to buy.

If someone invented antigravity (or discovered it, and then invented a mechanism for capturing it), would we invest and would it overtake anything we would be working on? I took antigravity as an example. It could be nuclear fusion. Or a way of reversing aging. Or a new way of making money while you sleep.

Well, yes, I think that would shake everything up so much that the latest idea you had would be eclipsed in attention. An idea on paper, as in an article in Nature, might not be enough to cut it for this boom unless a demonstration with a likely application was forthcoming and could conceivably be ramped up. I have seen, for example, the manuscript for Einstein's' $e=mc^2$ document, for example. But it wasn't even a proven theory until about 14 years after it was written and then the first application didn't come until 12 years after that.

Doesn't mean that there aren't customers for your service and that you can't make a steady cash flow from it, though.

The moral is that you have to move ahead with what you have, and allow for unexpected wonders to appear that might be something you can ally yourself with. Funny how many companies called themselves [something] technology, or dot com, bio-X, or –ics in the last booms.

Every boom is a little different from previous booms. We have already discussed how booms are similar, so now let's look at how this one will be special. One of the best ways to take advantage of booms is to find products and service-offerings that are at the intersection of several trends. I call this Boom Sex: the crossing of several trends together to make a new morphed thing.

The importance of the Story and Drivers and SubDrivers

Looking back at every boom, there seems to have been a really big Driver, or central match of pressures an enabler. The driver in the dotcom boom was obviously the Internet. The boom of 2007 was a housing and financial boom. Sometimes it is obvious what the central theme is, and you will want to build the story of your company around that if you want to get the funds and interest. Sometimes it is clear only in retrospect. For example, there is pretty much always a housing boom in the US and the UK in a boom. And financial services always do well in a boom. Perhaps what that means is that after the dotcom crash there was no explicit central driver?

Behind each driver is a sub driver. Plenty of money can be made in SubDrivers as they can be related to the main story of the driver and can be more specialized, somewhat invisible for a while and sometimes protected from the sheer sexiness of the main driver companies.

Even if you cannot align yourself with a driver or sub driver there is still plenty of room to benefit. In the dotcom days, housing went up and there was money to be made. High end clothing and party planning and restaurants and expensive wines all benefited.

Follow the money is a key rule for understanding booms. Money is a special thing in booms. Follow the Money! Money provides a store of value, a score, enabler, lubricant, and an equalizer. The flow of money is eased in a boom. Actually it is the credit rather than money itself you should be following. Making things happen take money. You have to get access to it. You can either have it beforehand, earn it, or born with it. (Or inherit it). If you earn it then your customer has to either have it beforehand, earn it himself, borrow it, or inherit it. There is a time lag on most of these processes, and so the timing of supply of money is important. And needs to be matched to the demand for money, i.e. How you will use it.

There is an enormous growth in demand for money, a much greater velocity as it flows around the economy.

Money can itself be seen like a product. It has a price and that price is affected by supply and demand.

Cyclical Growth Areas

Align with where growth is going to happen. Why is growth so important? If an area has no growth, then it will not need anymore resources. It is doing OK as it is. Growth areas need more service and products and need more people and software and financing. Ok, I exaggerate: some areas have been so cut that people are working unsustainably long hours and they will need some help.

Capital investment massively picks up in a recovery and boom. When companies see that there is true demand out there and to capture their share of these profit flows they need a machine or building, then they will invest. Construction, equipment, computers, machines all benefit. Anything that increases productivity, and quite a few that don't but still capture profit. With so much to play for, people will invest all the way up to marginal profitability.

People will open their wallets. They have more around, they won't miss a little more of it, they can't be bothered to argue and spend time over each incremental dollar bill. Therefore margins can be much higher in all sorts of businesses.

Herd instinct led by consumers. Even though consumers are relatively small direct investors, where they spend often leads to a bandwagon where institutional investors like pensions funds are forced to follow. Even if they don't agree. Let's see why. Retail investors can invest directly in the public companies they feel are good growth prospects. If those produce good returns, which they might if demand for their shares leads to a share price rise, then after a while consumers might ask why they are getting better results than their institutional investors. These institutional investors then are forced to follow the herd, however uninformed, in order to at least match the returns of the consumer investors. Hence a herd instinct is set up which becomes self-reinforcing.

I find the best framework to look at opportunities like this is to look at the top 5 trends in three areas: Desires, Pressures and Enablers. This is just one possible framework. This is why I believe it is a good way at looking at things:

I had thought about Needs, Wants and Enablers. But there is endless discussion about what is a need and what is a want indicating a fairly loose boundary between them. And then there are latent needs: things we tolerate and are not really aware of. A human being is a coping mechanism and we have to be kicked a bit to react, meaning latent need has to be dug out for it to be any use, but may in fact be powerful And what to do when a need is satisfied? Is it really satisfied? When a someone has a roof over their heads, they might start to look for entertainment or something creative to do. Or they might spend time trying to find a better roof to sleep under. So was their need really satisfied? It is easier to call these pressures and desires.

Economists says that demand leads to supply, and that entrepreneurs should look for needs to satisfy. This has been called "pull" marketing, as in the customers are pulling you. The opposite, "push" marketing is where you have a technology or product and you try to find uses for it. This is traditionally frowned upon. But, in reality, there is an interaction between what is possible to do and how we would like to use things.

Peter Drucker in his book "Innovation and Entrepreneurship" maintained that entrepreneurs need to look for areas of change. It is easier to expand into an area of change because demand tends to exceed supply and the existing players can't usually cope. People are open to new ideas and ways. I think this is fair, but an entrepreneur can also create a change and that can lead to growth.

Feel free to come up with your own framework. Let's look at these in turn. I give you my best guesses for what is new and different, and try to suggest ways you can look for opportunities in your area to customize the approach for you.

Here's my thinking:

Desires

All decisions are made by human beings. And their desires have not changed much over the centuries. Booms allow people to release their deepest desires. Therefore an opportunity will have to include human desires. They are the ones who buy and they buy what is best for them.

Pressures

When people make decisions, it is because they are under pressure from outside, or feel induced from inside. Inside is covered by desires. Outside is pressures. These pressures have to be new to stand a chance as a driver or sub driver. If they weren't new then there is a good chance that they would already have been satisfied.

Enablers

Originally, I termed this Technology. Technology seems to be the main root of growth in incomes so it seems be a key driver. The original Greek root of the word technology is "techne" which technically (sorry about the pun) means skill, so technology could be interpreted as new ways of doing things. But major innovations that change the world are not always new technologies but new ways of doing things. For example, you could argue that containerizing sea transport did not require a new technology per se: before and after you still used cranes and ships to offload. Making metal containers and carrying them on trucks was already being done. But containerization made globalization possible and increased incomes around the world massively. So think beyond technology to new ways of doing things.

Chapter 2.3: Desires

Booms are a time of self-expression, when you can be who you are truly are without fear.

Fantasies

Social acceptance is a powerful driver. Watch teenagers and their clothes at school. Watch the neighborhood cars in the driveways. We are influenced by what we know of successful and rich people. Newfound money in a boom allows to engage in fantasies like that. Or maybe you always craved being able to show that you made it when everybody wrote you off in your past. It's not a coincidence that Lehman traders in the years before the Lehman crash in 2008 possessed an average of 5 highly expensive watches.

The Seven Deadly Sins were a medieval creation designed to make all listeners pious and penitent. By labeling our baser desires, they hoped to prevent people sinking into them. But if they are baser desires and we believe that people will sink into them if allowed to, then we should examine them a bit better, shouldn't we, as a guide to what people will do? wrath, greed, sloth, pride, lust, envy, and gluttony.

Sloth. If you were rich would you take out the garbage, clean your shoes, book flights, or write memos? You would have someone do that for you. Or you might buy a product or app that saved you having to do it. Like flossing your teeth using a string is tricky so why not buy a small throwaway "violin bow" shaped thread holder to get the job done with less effort? Would you do an unpleasant job if you didn't have to? No, of course not. You would want to spend your time doing what you wanted.

Gluttony. A few weeks before the fall of the Berlin Wall (of course I didn't know it at the time), I went to visit East Berlin for a day. I was forced to buy some $6 worth of "Reichsmarks" and I knew I was expected to spend this money in the East side of the city. I tried some soup in a restaurant in the market square but that was awful. The grocery stores where empty. The best I could come up with was a large bowl of ice-cream (several pints worth) costing $3. Did I need 2 pints of ice-cream? No, but what the heck, it was cheap. I was richer than the local people and suddenly I could buy a lot. In a boom, when you are richer than before, you no longer need to limit yourself to smaller quantities, you can go for whatever you dream of. That's gluttony.

Wrath. People get angry because they get a payoff for being angry. It makes them feel good. It helps them gain release, and maybe because they enjoy exerting power over people. So being angry is a pleasure for some people! And so we would expect more people to be angry in a boom.

Greed and Pride. Greed and pride are very important motivators. As we can see from insider trading scandals, like Madoff, even though they clearly knew what they were doing was wrong, and they already had vast wealth, they continued to do illegal activities. They were greedy, they didn't want their lifestyle to stop and they were forced by their pride in achieving continued returns from ever stopping. They also knew that if they stopped and folded up their bags, they would reveal their wrongdoings.

Lust. In the wild days of Louis XIV, the courtiers at Versailles in France would eat vast delicacies, dress splendidly in powdered wigs and furred clothes, and take long naps, if you know what I mean.

In the 1960s, it wasn't just the time of the Pill and liberation, the sexual revolution happened because of the rejection of the conventions of before, and because human being's nature will out.

Envy. What could be more useful in a consumerist society than exciting envy in consumers? What does a rich Chinese or Russian businessman do when he has some money? Buy a top of the range foreign car to exhibit his wealth. Or buy real Louis Vuitton handbags from stores outside the country.

Maslow's Hierarchy is that wonderful triangle you may have seen that seeks to explain how people behave when their basic needs like food, shelter, sex and food are met. The theory is that you then seek to maximize your "self actualization." Nice theory. Not every one is the same and not everyone reacts the same way. Some people eat beans, live in a tent and follow their passion as painter or in a nonprofit. Others are motivated by keeping score of money and work to get rich, and then keep working hard at it. Others take more time off and don't work so hard. How to encompass all these different types of people? Maybe a way is to imagine the triangle is in fact a rubber bag like a pyramid full of water. The do-gooder is a slim bag that is extended upwards in a tall bag. The rich leisure-seeker is a bag that is fuller of water and so splayed out, with plenty of girth in the lower reaches of food, clothing, shelter etc. How to make this analogy for a boom? More boom, more wealth, more water in the bag. The rest is down to variation in human nature.

Comfort, security, reduced stress. People will pay for comfort. The world can be a harsh place. It can be hard to earn a living and provide for your family. Health worries, uncertainty at work, underfunded pensions can all provide a lot of stress. People will pay to have stress removed for their lives.

Childhood dreams. "Rosebud" was the last word of "Citizen Kane", the fictionalized biographical movie of Randolph Hearst, the newspaper magnate. A journalist, straining to hear his last words heard him say that word and spent the rest of the movie trying to discover its meaning. As you may know, Rosebud was the brand name of the snow sledge that as a boy he rode down a slope. And the whole movie's point was to show that even a rich and powerful man goes back to his most fun moments, and that was his childhood experience.

Childhood dreams are known to be powerful drivers in all of us, but they sometimes need to be released. A good way to think of what people do in a boom is to imagine a teenager with his daddy's credit card. Or, even better, a lottery winner.

What would they do? It's my theory that if we were released by more money, we would all follow childhood dreams, base desires, and experience sin. Ok, I might not be right all the way, since some people are wonderfully selfless. But let's start with that assumption and see where that leads us.
Ok you never became a firefighter, but you probably might admit that you crave the idea of being admired for your toughness, selfless and casual attitude to danger. Inside the financier is a firefighter dying to get out.

Now. People also want instant gratification. They want their pleasures now. Give them credit. It is no coincidence that most people buy their cars on a loan; it seems the only people who buy cars with cash these days are retired folk over 55. Everyone else does not want to wait until they are 55 to have a new car. The wide availability of credit cards and easier finance after the Second World War is often stated as a prime cause of the growth of the US Economy.

Value of time. If you are earning large amounts of money, you could either work longer hours to earn more money, or you could work less to have more time for leisure. Or, you could work more efficiently by outsourcing or delegating some of the work. That might mean a labor-saving product like a cordless drill, a faster-washing washing machine. And you could be more efficient and have more fun by outsourcing the work you don't want to do. That allows you to work hard, play hard, and earn hard.

Perfection
In austere times, people put up with less than perfection. Think of the spare design of furniture during the Second World War in Europe. In a boom, people feel they have a right to demand perfection.

They will eschew everyday brands when they can finally aspire to top brands. Why drink "Barefoot" sparkling wine when you could drink Perrier Jouet Champagne with a hand-painted flower on every bottle?

Me, Personalized. Why not have it your way? You can afford it and there are people to give you that.

Do good, feel good, look good. People like to feel good about themselves and with the average age of the population getting older, more and more people will feel a need to ensure a legacy of achievements. Philanthropy and volunteerism will increase.

Self-expressive. People will want to let their creative juices flow. When they are not worried about what other people think, because they have the money to feel secure, they will let it all hang out. They will make art, they will commission art, they will have their cars painted wild colors, they will have wild fantastic parties.

In another way, they will want to be seen to be up with the in-crowd and so they will spend on status-enhancing goods and services.

Would chrome fins on the back of automobiles have reached their highest point at any time other than a boom.)?

Other desires are: being connected, a desire for legacy, and of course making money.

Stories you can believe in. In the dotcom days, the Internet promised massive change to how people found out about products affecting marketing and distribution, among other things. This was a story believers could believe in.

In the late 1980s boom, the massive profits to be made from combining corporations and reducing costs caused by the availability of new capital led to a boom.

Further back, the 1960s booms were caused by more professional management massively impacting the performance of corporations.

Chapter 2.4: Pressures

Venture capitalists like to say they invest in companies that solve a problem that needs an "aspirin" not a "vitamin", i.e. a problem that causes significant pain for customers such that they are aware of their problem and actively searching for a solution. Nice thinking. Unfortunately it is obvious that not only do they not restrict themselves to aspirin problems, but that many successful stories are not in fact aspirin solvers.

I think a good way to look at opportunities is "Pressures, Desires, Enablers." Here's what I mean: pressures are like pain problems, fair enough. Desires tap into our deepest wants. Enablers are products that allow us to do something that we have been thwarted for some time, but have worked around or tolerated for some time. We may not be aware of these issues. And it may require a change of behavior to really make these enablers work, but they can find a rich vein. (Venture capitalists hate changes of behavior: they seem to take too long.) A quick example might be an Apple iPod which enables you to take your music collection with you, to just play your favorite songs, and to randomly play them.

Key thoughts on New Pressures

1. Is it new?

Firstly, the trend needs to be new. If not new, then sharply growing in importance. If it isn't new it is not going to be a driver of the boom, it will just be an enabler.

2. Does it apply to a fair number of people?

Secondly, the trend cannot be too new: it needs to be something that will be applicable to a reasonable number of users in a short period of time. It takes time for customers to accept new ways of doing things and with only 4 years to go, that might not be enough time. Malcolm Gladwell's the "Tipping Point" popularized the need for a new way to reach a critical mass before it might really take off. Believers need to believe that this new ways of using things can get to the tipping point. They look at this by looking at whether they adopt, whether people they trust adopt, how quickly adoption is happening, and how adoptable other people are likely to be.

3. Will it lead to big change? Thirdly, to be meaningful the potential for future usage needs to be large. This means large markets, lots of value, massive change in acceptance, or is likely to lead to much bigger things. As a rule of thumb I would suggest you look for changes more than 20% in the next 5 years.

4.Trends often have setbacks. Funny how people will try to persuade you that the only way is up with every trend. Heard the one about real estate: "they aren't making any more land"? True enough but that doesn't stop prices being overbid and then coming down.

5. How to discover more New Pressures. By the time a boom comes, it may be obvious what the pressures are that matter. But there might be a few pressures you can benefit from if you look harder. So how to find them?

One way to discover new pressures is to look at anything that might cause a problem and the look at whether that problem is meaningful inside the time of the next boom period.

New Pressures to look out for.
Here's my best guess for the top 5 social trends that will affect things over the next 5 years."

Demographics
There are three aspects of demography that matter: Populations shifts, people in developed countries retiring, and people in developing countries are very young.

Public sector deficits.
In the developed world, many of the public sector is even more in debt because of the financial crisis of 2007-2009 and the resulting recession. Deficits increased due to bailing out banks, spending even while revenues decreased due to lower

tax receipts because of lower economic activity, and due to expensive attempts to stimulate the economy. Spending cuts are in the future and so the public sector will struggle to fulfill politician's promises and voter expectations. This can be an opportunity in that the private sector can provide these services. Revenue can then be gained from consumers, businesses, or directly from the government itself.

One of my favorite examples of such public private partnership is JC Decaux which taking over the cleaning and investing in bus shelters in France. Private security firms like Blackrock have been outsourced to in the Iraq.

Resource Shortages. Oil
Water and many commodities will be in short supply as economies recover and delving countries develop.

The "Supercycle" theory and peak oil theories all posit that prices must go up as demand from Asia drives demand upwards faster than supply can be found and that we are running out.

Most developed countries actually are seeing negative population growth and diminishing intensity of usage per capita, which means less resources are being used.

Growth of China and BRICS
The biggest change in wealth is going to be in Asia and developing countries. Aspirational wealth will be caused by access to credit.

Let's try to understand what is happening over there. Clearly the Developed world is buying a lot of products from China. This has massively accelerated since 2000 when China was admitted to the World Trade Organization. American and Developed World wealth is therefore accruing to the vast number of small enterprises as well as state companies. This wealth is being saved, spent and invested. The Chinese government, during the Great Recession, pumped some

$2000bn into infrastructure in order to stimulate the economy and keep it going as the Developed World dropped off, and to invest for the future. This money then trickles down throughout the economy. So now they are developing a solid middle class which earns good money. Wage increases are of the order of 12% per year This rising tide is lifting all boats; some 200m have been lifted out of poverty in just ten short years. These people all aspire to a greater standard of living and they will make purchase to get it.

For example, it is well known that poor people eat beans and other cheap protein. As they become richer they move up to meat and that is what is happening in China. The same will apply to consumer products and services.

Climate Change
This being a "tragedy of the commons" problem, where individually we cannot easily influence the outcome for the good, the major forces to cause such externalities to be solved are legislation or subsidies. Legislation, as in the State of California, which mandates that 50% of energy will be from renewable sources by 2030, imposes a cost on California voters and citizens in terms of increased costs. Subsidies, means that tax revenues are diverted to reduce the price to the consumer or to increase the profit of the producer while maintaining price. Voluntary price increases, such as buying a less polluting product, are only really accepted by a small part of the population at moment.

Failed States and Nuclear Proliferation
It is easy to ignore a pressure and not consider it as an opportunity. Unless it comes across as a trend in the right direction that you can solve and exploit. But there are many problems which are pressures that could be opportunities if you can solve them and find ways to capturing the value. Failed states and nuclear proliferation seem like too big for us to solve in a meaningful way at a capitalist level, but they cannot be ignored as they are big and powerful pressures.

Chapter 2.5: Enablers

Human beings love quick fixes and get rich quick schemes. And technology has been the solution for many centuries. Especially in America. It is the way we look at the world, and the way we thinking of solving problems. It may not be right, but it is a bet that this is a valid approach that will continue for some time.

In Silicon Valley, like a hammer that only sees things as nails or not-nails, technology is the answer to everything and the search for the next technology is all. But the last boom did not have technology as its main driver. And financial engineering and new business models can sometimes be enough to build SubDrivers. So don't be obsessed by the technology.

Now, it is possible that someone will invent antigravity, a portable nuclear fusion energy source, a way of increasing longevity of humans. And it is possible that might be a key driver for the next boom. But I think not. Technologies like this rarely appear fully gestated. They take time to be nurtured. Not to say that there isn't a research lab somewhere in the world which has invented or discovered something. And it would be a good idea to go through Nature, Scientific American, Wired, New Scientist and other magazines and journals from the last 5 years to look for these developments.

We all know that failure rates for new to the world devices are very high. Something that really will get adopted quickly will score highly on the "ACCTO" scale. Originated and modified by Everett Rogers, new ideas achieve quickest adoption if they have: high relative Advantage, Compatible with existing ways of doing things, Complexity: not so complex no one can use them, Trialability: it's easy to try and test things out, Observability: you can plainly see the advantages.

I would probably make Isaac Newton turn in his grave if I were to say that inertia is a very powerful social force, but it takes a big obvious advantage sometimes to make people want to try something new.

Key thoughts on New Enablers

1. Is it new but useable? Secondly, the trend cannot be too new: it needs to be something that will be applicable to a reasonable number of users in a short period of time. It takes time for customers to accept new ways of doing things and with only 4 years to go, that might not be enough time. Malcolm Gladwell's the "Tipping Point" popularized the need for a new way to reach a critical mass before it might really take off. Believers need to believe that this new ways of using things can get to the tipping point. They look at this by looking at whether they adopt, whether people they trust adopt, how quickly adoption is happening, and how adoptable other people are likely to be.

2. Only can use what is on shelf

For a key driver, technology is not likely to be totally mature but it has to be beyond a prototype and not too far from the market to make it work. There have to be companies which are public for investors to invest in. Chances are, the technology has not quite "crossed the chasm." That is, early adopters are using it and the potential is to sell the product to the rest of us.

For a SubDriver, the technology has to be on the shelf and usable without extensive customization. This technology needs to be like a cordless drill: people know how to use it and it is reliable. In technology terms, it must have "crossed the chasm" for early adopters.

If we look at the dotcom days, the browser existed but only in a rough form as Mosaic then in better form as Netscape Navigator which was usable by all of us. In the background, the internet plumbing had existed for quite sometime, even decades.

So a totally revolutionary technology idea outlined in an article, like how you might combine DNA strands would not quite be enough to spark a driver if it has never been achieved in the lab and there is no easy route to product ionization.

The world is filled with massive inertia which prevents massive change quickly. Safety legislation on new vehicles, understanding of risks of genetically modified foods, time to build awareness of climate change, are all examples. While not neglecting the immense power of consumer demand when so moved, and the lobbying power of an industry big enough to provide meaningful employment and reward, there is barely enough time for this boom to happen with anything that is not on the shelf and readily deployable.

Thomas Kuhn, in his book "The structure of Scientific Revolutions" argues that new paradigms could take 25 years to become adopted, the same time as a generation of administrators to retire and make way for newer-trained people.

3 Has to be on stock market or investable.
A boom can be defined as ballooning flows of money and credit. What makes it move is the hope of a good return or yield. Since ownership is critical to owning a return then boom must generate vehicles whose price is transparent, where ownership is clear and legal, where your part of it can easily be turned back into money (i.e. liquidity), which can absorb enough capital, and, where needed, can provide more capital for these companies to grow.

If demand is sufficiently high then some of these requirements can be waived. Hence the surge into social networking private companies like Facebook and LinkedIn in the early 2010s. Hence their willingness to buy into media and internet media companies like Google with dual share ownership structures (i.e. your share gets almost less voting power than the management).

Exchange traded commodities, the opening of the Chinese stock market through Hong King, that many non-US shares are quoted in dollars, all indicate the desirability of these traits.

In the biotech eighties, the biotech companies went public in IPOs to capture this demand, and to allow investors and management to realize their gains. In the railway boom, similarly.

4. Will it lead to big change

Thirdly to be meaningful the potential for future usage needs to be large. This means large markets, lots of value, massive change in acceptance, or is likely to lead to much bigger things. As a rule of thumb I would suggest you look for changes more than 20% in the next 5 years.

How do you figure out how big a change could be caused? Imagine you have a new paint technology that allows metallic paint on cars. It might become a big fad (actually it was in the later 1970s) but it's not world-changing.
Imagine you are a new free email service. Would that change the world? Possibly, but the barriers to entry are low and there is very little business model for making money, and the idea is not revolutionary (any more). So it is unlikely.

5. All older technologies fight back against new technologies by improving their performance.

Older technologies stand to lose if eclipsed by newer technologies. The companies supporting them will lose out. So they will be highly motivated to fight back. In Foster's "Innovation Advantage" he shows that throughout history many older technologies are motivated to reinvent themselves and evolve in order to survive. This has the effect of delaying or nullifying the impact of a new technology. This could prevent a technology becoming a driver of a boom.

You can see this with wind power. New technologies and the discovery of shale natural gas allows the supply of natural gas to go up, the price to compete down, and the newer technologies of wind power are struggling to compete.

6. Avoid being sold a bill of goods
Or think about wind and solar power. Hyped since the 1973 oil crash, they went into abeyance and then have been resurrected as the next great hope. But several large solar panel companies have been going bust. How can that be? It is because of four things: competitors saw a big market and came into the industry, because energy costs are still above the costs of producing with coal or oil (which means they need subsidies to exist), and they require investment above plugging devices into the sockets (which requires capital for investment and a payback period).

An enabler does not have to have a decent business model to be an enabler in a boom, but it sure helps. The bio industry has been absorbing venture capital for some 40 years but only recently has it earned a return for investors as an industry.

My good friend, Anton Milner, with whom I was at Business school, was CEO of QCells, the largest manufacturer of solar cells in the world for some time, and valued at 48bn. They had to close plants and their very existence is at stake.

Advertizing and free are the last refuge of the weak business models. (but Google).

7. Exciting
The boom is likely to be driven by something retail investors find exciting. Why is this? They have funds that can move quickly and like a herd and they are more susceptible to "stories." They are more desperate for yield. They follow price trends and jump quickly. When most fund managers can barely approach the average return of the index, retail investors think they can do better by being more active. If prices go up in a certain asset then they will invest more. And then other retail investors will place their fund managers under pressure to be in those assets whose prices are

appreciating, even if there is no reliable rationale. Funds will be pulled out of funds which "do not get it"; some will be forced to close. The herd instinct pervades the whole investment industry, driven by retail investors with their large discretionary investable income.

8. Diminishing Returns and Reversion to Mean
The law of diminishing returns states that the more you do something, i.e. the less the effect from every unit for effort. In other words the effect tails off. Or, the biggest effects often happen at the start. So for example, when people say that within 30 years China will take over the world or everyone on the planet will have a cell phone, they haven't allowed for the increased difficulty of reaching everyone and that some people will never have one.

Reversion to mean indicates that most sudden upwards trends tend towards their historical average sometime later. I.e. Most sudden trends are not sustainable.

9. Build on previous work.
Previous booms have ended so suddenly that the discovery of a new pressure and a new enabler to satisfy it may have died early. However it may not quite have been developed right but the oxygen it needed to adapt was cut off. That does not mean that it could not flourish today. So it is important not to discount "failed" technologies and underexploited pressures.

10. How to discover more New Enablers
The fun thing about making predictions is guessing where you are going to be wrong. Because you will be, as I am! So you will have to discover other drivers and enablers not on this list.

The science fiction author William Gibson said that "the future is already here, it's juts not widely distributed yet". This means the ideas that are ready for prime time are already working somewhere and just need to be found, adapted and brought to the market.

One way to discover new enablers is to look at anything that might solve a problem and then try to see whether the problem it might solve could be meaningful and marketable inside the time of the next boom period.

New Enablers to look out for

Communication/Mobile/ Sensors/Computing/language software

Many people do not understand that the biggest usage of computers is not in fact in "computing" as in calculating formulae, but in communications. When computers first began to be available commercially they were used for calculating, designing bombs and figuring to how much to elevate a gun to hit an object 3 miles away, and in controlling automatic transmissions in cars. [1] IBM figured there would be a need for maybe 6 computers in the whole world. Nowadays you can have 60 just in your car. When it comes to communications, there are an endless number of calculations that need to be performed on every bit of information. Hence computers are mainly used in communications.

Energy and Climate

The planet seems to be getting warmer and many people believe this is due to human emissions mainly to do with carbon fuels. Climate technology aims to reduce carbon emissions, scrub the atmosphere and provide less-carbon intensive ways of generating power.

The three key problems with climate technology seem to be that they mostly cost more than the equivalent carbon fuels to a consumer, and they often rely on additional investment, and they often suffer from drawbacks compared to existing fuels. It is true that many of the costs of cleanup are not fully included in the price of carbon fuels. However this means that adoption of such energy sources is reliant on subsidies and tax

[1] Did you know that until 1974 automatic transmissions were the dominant form of nonhuman intelligence on the planet?

breaks from governments, regulations forcing adoption, or the goodwill of consumers.

Saving energy, or using the equivalent of "negenergy," is definitely a useful idea, though often further investment is required.

Could a boom be started from climate technology? Or, know what you are thinking. Oil is on the way out, how can it be a driver of a new boom?

Secondly there have been several rapid changes in technology in the last decade which have totally reversed trends. Being able to extract more gas, being able to take oil from shale, being able to extract oil from tar sands, being able to drill horizontally. They have all changed the dynamics of where oil is produced and the whole pricing. Natural gas in the US for example is much cheaper than expected because of the large quantities of shale gas discovered. Countries that thought they would be importing gas are now exporting. This is making several alternative energy sources such as wind uncompetitive.

Even if industry is a growing one, there may be no profits for the companies involved. The airline industry is well-known one in which the industry has cumulatively lost money since the Wright Brothers.

Other ideas are; *Materials, Bio/DNA/Food, New Sources of Capital*

Boom Sex: Cross-pollinating to make new mutations
Imagine organizing a series of tunnels between cages in which animals called "new uses" and "new doings" are kept. They travel among themselves and latch onto each other and begin to mate.

How to spot if things are not going to plan

"The best laid schemes o' mice an' men
Gang aft a-gley, [often go awry]
An' lea'e us nought but grief an' pain"
Robert Burns.

Having an idea of what the future might hold is the key to taking advantage of it. However, you can be sure that nothing will work to quite how you expect. If the boom does not appear to be materializing then you will need to make some downside protection plans. Being overleveraged being late to the party, being unprepared for recession or shocks can all wreck your plans. So the key is to be prepared for shocks and events not transpiring as you might expect. Maybe the boom is arriving sooner than you thought. How would you change your plans?

There are several methods of minimizing problems:
Firstly, keep a weather eye out for changes. Expect the shocks, external events, the unexpected. Learn to compare your ideas against what is happening. What indicators are going to be good early warning signs? Make sure you keep an eye on the leading, not lagging indicators.

Secondly, avoid making bet-the-company deals. I recognize that may not be possible. Waiting too long could be disastrous, too.

Thirdly, have an endgame plan worked out. Booms don't peter out, they crash and burn. Suddenly and often without warning. Therefore you need to not try to be too clever about timing your exit of your endgame.

Fourthly, when you are about to do something ask yourself whether you would look foolish doing this is in 2 years' time, say, there was a recession. You'd be amazed how often this might stop you spending your savings frivolously, buying a company, taking on too much debt.

Part 3: Boom Strategy

We've established, I hope, that a boom is going to happen, and tried to explain what happens in a boom. In this section we work on ways for you to take advantage of a boom, and your knowing earlier than most that it is likely to happen.

Why you need a personal boom strategy The aim of the book is to get you to look 10 steps ahead and work out how to take advantage of what is coming your way. Have you thought about your personal boom strategy? What are you going to do to take advantage of the upcoming boom?

As Kennedy reminded us there are perils of action and perils of inaction. You could compare anything you might think about doing with a "wait and see" or "do nothing" strategy. Usually things work out better when you have a plan. As Clausewitz said: no plan survives contact with the enemy" but as Patton: a plan vigorously executed is better than a plan in a week."

You as business, investor and consumer.
You yourself are a business, an investor and a consumer. You earn, invest, and spend. So is your company. So is your customer. So is the government. You need to see everything through the eyes of each party through these three lenses.

Let's take a look at how you can benefit in each of these areas of your life, while taking into account what happens in a boom and what is special about the net boom/.

As a service provider, you provide a service in return for money. That's what you do to earn a living. Even if you are in manufacturing, you are really a service-provider. You may operate a machine (=provide a service) making a product but you are really a service provider. In the end the customer doesn't care whether you deliver a cordless drill and drill but which he uses to drill a hole in a piece of wood, or whether you turn up at his house and use a cordless drill to make a ole for him. They are equivalent services.

We are all self-employed, in a way, now. You're selling yourself and what you can do every day (well, if you're onto it). You could do nothing. The boom will come to you eventually and things will be happier. What could you do, apart from nothing new, to take advantage of the boom? You could gain more money by specializing and marketing yourself as an expert. You could be a generalist who gets things done. You could increase your skills and earn more money from your existing customers, Or you could look for other customers who might want to buy your services. Or maybe both, where your new skills could get you into new markets.

As a consumer, well, you could consume! Yes, yes, more retail therapy! Perhaps you like travel or vacations. Or buying collector's items. Or getting around to that hobby or sport you like. You could finally get that snowmobile or yacht. Might have to save first though, so better start now.

As an investor, we invest to build security, and to grow our assets. To be safe and to be richer and freer. Investing and saving are equivalent in that they are not spending. But people don't save much these days. And when they do, those savings can be used to consumer or invest.

Chapter 3.1: General Boom Strategy

Here are my top 5 picks for the next boom:
Marketing Services
Everybody wants to get their voice heard, their story told, their brand recognized, and their products and services bought. The enormous increase in supply of alternatives will flood the market and confuse the mind. Marketing services companies and products that make it possible to stand out somehow will be in massive demand. Much money will be spent on it.

Think advertising, PR, word of mouth campaigns, giving away products that people normally pay for, experiences.

Think off the wall, new technologies, outrageousness.

Financial Services and products
Everybody is going to be making money, especially those with money! They will want to make more of it. They will be desperate for yield and managing risk at the same time.

It is traditional for sectors close to those with money to make more money than most of us. Their results (even if not their contribution) can usually be easily measured.

Think new derivatives, derivatives on derivatives, exchange traded substitutes, synthetic anything, options, annuities, insurance, risky hedging.

They are easy to develop and fast to diffuse.

Productivity Services and Products
Everyone is making money and they are busy making more if it. They want tools to make more of it. They also want to enjoy their leisure time more therefore they want productivity tools to increase their ability to make more money and use les time.

Hence the prevalence for schemes to "make money while you sleep".

Filofax, time management training, word processors, PowerPoint, were all diffused during booms. Think new forms of stimulant like coffee.

Having a good time.
We are all feeling rich and happy and safe and secure. We love life and we want to drink deep.

Think parties, experiences like travel, drugs, art. Especially anything which can done quickly to fit in around work, such as portable gaming, quick getaways vacations, short release drugs.

Niche Services
More people are willing to spend more money to get what they want, without the normal hassle. This sets up the boom as the perfect time for startups in niche services.

Three factors are a stake here:
People are becoming wealthy; they have money to spend and are willing to do so.

They are enjoying themselves and don't want to do boring, menial, or low status tasks. Therefore they are willing to pay to offload boring or inconvenient tasks.

Because they are earning plenty of money, their opportunity cost of doing anything other than their specialized job is high: they could earn a whole lot more doing what they do best.

Think dog-walking, tax preparation.

Baby boomers, as they retire and approach retirement, still being in good health, as they have newly-built-up portfolios, will want to self-actualize.

Many people will to realize that the boom is short-lived and will see it as the new normal. Therefore they will happily invest vast sums of money for there future, based on unrealistic expectations. This can be exploited by education services for example. Advice on how to earn more money will be immensely leveraged. So think investing tips.

When the visibility of high earnings is apparent, as for example, people spending $100 on a bottle of wine in a restaurant, then people will move into those fields. Financial services always do very well in a boom, for example.

Think bigger

Booms are times of new products, new markets, new ways of doing things and times of surpluses. They are times to think bigger and make wild achievements happen. Credit is the fuel on which you can reach the stratosphere. This is much more available in a boom.

New products, services and markets

People are willing to try new things more than ever before. New products and services could massively increase their productivity in making more money or in reducing the time taken to do nonearning functions. People are willing to pay because their opportunity cost is so high.

An analogy I like to make compared the opportunity costs of an unemployed man and a busy executive who both want to have their house painted. The busy man knows that every hour of his time is worth a lot of money. He doesn't get enough time with his kids and wife and doesn't take all of his vacation time. This means his spare time has an even higher opportunity cost. He is willing to pay someone to do the job. The unemployed man, however, has no real value to his time. He also may be short of money. He will do the painting himself. In a boom we all move from being underemployed and earning below our potential to busy people with costs to every minute.

Another way to look at this, in case you are not convinced, is that of a lawyer who has an assistant to prepare documents and do photocopying. Even though the lawyer could do her documents better, it is definitely in her interest to stand up in court and leave the paperwork to her assistant. Newly wealthy Asian middle class and Russian business people, for example, exhibit the same behavior.

New business models
Some people will demand more services for less money in certain less interesting sectors because they can free money up for discretionary purchases they would rather spend their money on. This explains the apparent cheapness of some rich people. The key is to present your service or product as saving their time and having little competition in those key areas. Or using a different way of charging people that appeals to their self-interest.

Look out for shocks
Planning for the unforeseeable is essential! Shocks come in two flavors: the totally unexpected, and the expected that fails to materialize. Which is more important is for you to judge. Let's look at them both in turn.

a. Totally unexpected shocks. "There are known knowns. There are things we know that we know. There are known unknowns. That is to say, there are things that we now know we don't know. But there are also unknown unknowns. There are things we do not know we don't know."

It is the left field shock that is the hardest to figure out. Not only may its existence be hard to spot but the extent of its impact is unknown.

One possible way of minimizing these side impacts is to "send out scouts" to look out for the unexpected, to know what areas of the business are the most vulnerable, and to guard those.

b. The Expected that fails to materialize. "It ain't what you don't know that gets you into trouble. It's what you know for sure that just ain't so." Mark Twain

Here you know what to look for and are ready tracking it. And you can figure out the impact should something happen. Of course you are likely to be busy and working on assumptions and so surprise events may take you by surprise!

Perhaps the best way to avoid being blindsided by these shocks is to write down assumptions and figure out what indicators show. Or they remain valid and check them occasionally.

How Booms End

How to spot the ending of the Boom

I.e. How can you spot a recession coming? Since booms end suddenly and often due to an unexpected shock, you could argue that you will not therefore be able to spot the end before it happens. I agree a bit and disagree mostly. The atmosphere is exceedingly exuberant and you will have seen it before. This is the time like just before the Crash of 1929 when shoeshine boys were giving stock hints. I remember my realtor in 1989 trying to sell me house; he was 23 and had just bought a house I was coveting and I had been working for a lot longer than he had and I was in high-paying job.

The exact timing will probably not be predictable, both because its likely cause will not be apparent, and because the possible causes that are apparent cannot easily be understood.

But do all booms end in recessions?

Yes. There are so many excesses built up in a boom that a quiet whimper or slow deflation of a bubble is very rare indeed. The Fed tries to manage this to avoid a big recession by "removing the punchbowl just as the guests start drinking."

And can't you have a recovery without a boom?

Good question. I think not, though you might have a recovery where the boom was "cut off" because a large shock came along and ended the recovery before it got to boom.

Can you have a boom that doesn't end in a recession?
In other words, can we have a boom that gently peter out or stays steady rater than ending in a violent crash? I think this is unlikely. The Fed would like to engineer things this way and the government would certainly like that. The Fed's policy is to ensure steady conditions to provide a stable business climate.

Booms represent a massive excess of so many things that the massive imbalances cannot easily be dissipated; they grow and grow and no one can see an end to them. Too many people are individually invested in their continuance that they will not allow themselves to be stopped from pursuing their goals. It appears that the only way for them to stop is for them to be stopped by a big external event, an explosion, a recession.

Getting YOUR Timing right

Timing matters in two ways: things take time to manifest, and you need to match your entry and exits with the environment around you.

Living in California near the beach I see surfers all the time. And they teach me that understanding waves of business cycles are like surfing. You have to look over your shoulder, sense a buildup and start accelerating so that when the wave comes by you are well-matched and you can ride the wave. As anybody who has ever surfed can tell you, getting the timing wrong means you come to the surface spluttering for air. Same thing with a boom. Miss it and you are struggling. Let's see if we can all read the signs and get the timing right.

Supply and Demand
Timing does matter, not only in coordinating with events around you, but also because things take time to make happen. Just like surfing where you need time to get speed up, so you need time while you get things ready for a boom. Imagine you want to buy a house. You need time to get some savings put aside for a deposit, you need time to build up good credit, you need time to find the right place. Launching a new product or service? You need time for new customers to hear about the product, try it and tell others about it. In many cases, things get bigger by compounding, that is results feed off results. All these things take time. So you can't wait until the boom is upon you, you need to start thinking now about what you can achieve and when to get going.

Assets for sale are liable in separate peaks. The first is at the end of the recession, the second is in boom time. Let's look at why this is. At the end of a recession, if a company or individual is overextended then he may choose to sell. If he is short of cash flow, he will try to sell at any price. If the bank owns the assets they may choose to sell now at any price or delay to get a better price. Entities tend to run out of cash at the end of the recession. Like a car going around a corner a little too fast, they come off the road at the latter stages of the curve. With companies and individuals, they have been trying to conserve cash but they finally run of road and crash. This can clearly be a good time to buy, if you have the cash. Sometimes owners will delay to the start of the recovery to get higher prices, and this can also be a good time to buy.

However, most assets are available in a boom period. Why is this? It is because companies restructure to focus and to put their capital into assets they can make more money out of, and because they believe there are people out there who are willing to pay top dollar for those assets, and because they are showing fabulous performance (usually because they are cyclical businesses that do well in a boom). The other thing is that the buyers finally have money to burn at the boom. Clearly, buying assets at the end of the boom would be a bad time to buy, if you can help it. Buyers are often naive about the business cycle and think the boom will go on for ever. Many of the owners of assets can see the end of the boom and are aware of the performance of their companies in a recession.

So the role of timing is to understand the supply/demand position and plan for it by accessing capital earlier in the cycle.

Price of a "thing" seems to be governed by 4 aspects: Supply (how much is being made available every day), demand (how much people want it), how much of it is in inventory and therefore readily available to soak up any surprising demand, and how much money is flowing in speculatively. The latter has to do with expectations of prices, the alternatives, and the amount of money or credit flowing around looking for a return.

Exit Strategies

Some boom strategies rely on you to exit before a recession to maximize your returns. It is therefore not enough to time your entry, you also have to time your exit. And that takes looking forward, flexibility and planning.

Missing the exit time can be painful and loss-making. Imagine if you were still invested n the stock market in 2008. The stock market went down some 40%, though it did bounce back by early 2011, about 2 years later. You could have saved yourself two years of going nowhere. And if you had borrowed against your equity, you might well have run out of cash and be forced to sell at short notice in a fire sale, losing almost everything.

Many companies are bought at the end of the boom on debt. If they are cyclical businesses whose revenues fall 40% in a recession and have high fixed costs, the interest burden can sink the company.

We have all heard of people who earned fabulous amounts for a company and then had to plow it all back in to keep the thing going through the recession which followed.

Chapter 3.2: For Entrepreneurs and Business Owners

Some strategies:

1. Build a business aligned with major drivers

The attention and credit will go mainly to those areas aligned with the major derivers in the boom. While allowing for competition which is also driven into that area, it makes sense to be closely aligned and be able to tell your story as being linked to the drivers.

2. Delegate your work as much as possible

You need to get the maximum productivity out of your time as possible. So you need to use IT, hire people, build a management and rewards structure, and use your strengths to set up new business initiatives.

3. Choose a business you can get out for you to realize the value

Your time is the most precious commodity you have. If it is all consumed in the business and the business will not function without you then you have become trapped and cannot release the true value of your work. You need to structure the business that you can sell it or it will run without you being present every second.

4. Plan for massive ramp-up and start now.
It takes time to achieve things. It takes time for brand recognition. It takes time to build up the relationships with your bank to get credit. It takes time to nurture customer relationships. It takes time to build a team which can function well. So you need to start now.

The boom is short so you need to be ready for when it "hits" or you will miss the boat. Remember the surfing analogy: if you aren't well-positioned and looking over your shoulder for the oncoming wave, it will pass over you.

5. Plan for a recession
Don't forget that all booms end in a recession caused by a shock. It is only a few years away so allow for that, with an exit strategy, a hiring strategy that allows you to turn down the volume, and a debt strategy that doesn't use up all your assets.

Chapter 3.3: For Managers and Employees

1. Help guide the business towards drivers

Your company will massively benefit from being positioned in a driver area and you will benefit as an employee, therefore it makes sense to redirect efforts towards those drivers.

2. Use productivity-enhancing tools and delegate

Companies exist for their shareholders, their employees and of course their customers. Given the presence of competition everyone needs to see massive productivity for everyone to get rich and not be passed-by. It is your job to massively leverage everyone's efforts and assets.

3. Outsource anything that could be done outside.

When the rush happens there will be precious little time to get everything done. Lower level activities that slow down producers should be minimized and sent to cheaper resources. This may mean outsourcing, automating, or eliminating.

4. Allow for talent wars and look after people.

In a boom, demand for talent will exceed supply. The boom is so quick that people cannot easily be found to fill all the gaps. Your workers will be in demand and will know it. They will start to realize their value and will ask for more money or will leave to companies who realize that they can earn more money if they hire more and better workers.

In the dot com craze, tech companies were so desperate for people that you could earn $1000 for recommending a new hire who was subsequently taken on.

For employees

1. Get into a field that will benefit from massive drivers

Masses of money will be showered on fields related to key drivers. Employers will face a talent war. You need to position yourself in the right fields. Maybe invest in yourself and do a quick retraining and get into the right field early and your earnings will massively benefit as a result.

2. Do a good job and show how you are productive

Funny how books that advise people on getting a good job seem to mention "doing a good job" only in passing. But that is what an employer wants more than anything else. Or do a good job and make sure that you are recognized for it. If the employer can easily figure out how productive you are, and how much he is earning from your time then he can readily see who you might be worth more.

3. Ask for salary raises

Which means you can ask for higher salary and benefits.

4. Consider being self-employed

If you have organizational and business development skills then you should be able to capture a bigger margin on your time by being self-employed. In a boom, there are numerous opportunities for high margin service businesses which do not require much capital to get going. Why not start plotting now and be up and running for the boom?

Chapter 3.4: For Consultants & Service-Providers

Here are four strategies:

Develop expertise and market to a field which will be massively aligned with drivers. One of the obvious reasons consultants are hired is for their specialist expertise, so see if we can develop some quickly in an area aligned with a growth driver. Read all the books, go to courses, work for someone in that field,. Write a book, market to the right people.

Allow clients to outsource to you. Another reason consultants are hired is that they provide a ready resource when they are short of resource, You can get things done and they want to offload nonproductive tasks, as well as get their organization going ion the right direction.

Delegate to new people and reward. In your organization it makes sense for you to delegate and outsource nonearning activities, so you can maximize your time on the best-producing areas.

As a service provider, you could take over jobs your boss or your company or your client don't want to do. EDS did this by managing computer systems that companies didn't want to do. TurboTax does this for tax preparation. How can you help your business take advantage of the boom?

How can you take advantage of the boom in the company? Since the company will be more profitable, you should be able to negotiate higher pay. As the company grows you should be taking on greater responsibilities, so salary and bonuses should increase. Your seniority will also increase.

What's happening around you
Your customers are getting richer, more concerned about their time, want to earn more. You are getting richer, more concerned about time, and want to earn more.

Everybody is getting richer. This means they can spend more money, they are willing to try new methods of making more money.

Everybody wants to earn more for their time. This means they are willing to pay to maximize the effectiveness of their time. As a consultant or employee or employer this means you can profitably take on jobs they don't want to do. It also means that you can outsource the bits you don't want to do. It also means you will have to pay your workers more.

Chapter 3.5: For Investors and Home Owners

With massive debts, most people are worried about running out of cash before they die. The boom will take care of a lot of that. However Medicare and Social Security remain in massive deficit. Therefore investors will, in contrast to the usual advice, be forced to amp up the risk on their portfolios to try to get better yields. This is a ride you need to get onto as well.

1. For home-owners

After every recovery there is always a home boom. Always. People are wealthy, feel wealthy and have access to cheap credit. Housing is highly leveraged and has fantastic tax advantages. And of course you get the benefit of enjoying it personally. Housing tends to increase over time. Therefore housing is likely to be the preferred investment vehicle of US as individuals for sometime to come.

If you are not on the housing ladder then now would be a good time to get in. Start saving, look for those 104% mortgages which will soon be available, and build credit.

Many people invest in second homes but these are virtually unsellable in a recession. Rental properties are much more stable in earnings (though less fun!)

2. For stock investors

It is quite obvious that the stock market has a self-fulfilling effect going on: if the price is going up, more investors will climb aboard and the price will continue to go up. So, in investing we all go with the herd (i.e. we can get in early enough) and then leave before the herd.

Chapter 3.6: For You, Personally

So, how to put it all together? Let's see where we are now. We started by looking at why an economic boom is coming, despite our doubts, and why a good guess would be 2016. We learned how booms work and what makes them self-reinforcing and grow. We looked at their essential characteristic and how they are very different from recessions ands recoveries. Then we speculated on possible major drivers and enablers that would drive the next boom. We are now in a position to come up with an action plan for taking advantage of te next boom for ourselves.

Remembering that we are all service providers, investors and consumers, let's work on strategies in each of these three areas of our lives.

Conclusion

"Boom Ahoy!" is a book designed to provoke you a little into contemplating how your life might be different if you cold plan and take advantage of an upcoming boom. Which I think is coming soon and faster than you think/. I could be wrong on things and what I think are drivers and enablers. You have your own ideas. I hope that together we have been able to learn techniques to look 10 steps ahead. But even looking up and seeing one step ahead is better than nothing and will put you ahead of most of your fellow-travelers. I hope you enjoy the journey!

P.S. Don't forget that booms are short, and they are always followed by recession, so plan now.

Appendices

Appendix 1: Perils of Prediction

You might think that, given the way society ridicules people whose predictions are wrong that no one would ever make a prediction. It might be only crazy fools like myself.

Problem is, if you don't look up when you walking down a sidewalk, you are quite likely to run into a post. Or a ditch. If you look too far up the road, you might also run into a ditch. So the key is to look ahead far to gauge the lie of the land and then look closer. It makes me sign when I think how little I knew about life and careers when I left school. Leading a sheltered childhood meant several of my classmates were able to see opportunities further than I was, opportunities that, when they came by me, I was not positioned to grab hold of. Same thing with how to plan for a boom.

I urge you to take on the main thrust of this book, which is that an economic boom is coming towards you faster than you might imagine and that, by realizing that, you can take advantage of it.

For some people it is less intimidating if you don't think of prediction so much as putting a date on an event, but more as looking into the future and developing a vision of what might be.

Many companies, for example, have a go at outlining scenarios, that is, alternative likelihoods. I like to think of it as imagining the landscape of a city you have never been to. You have heard a bit about that city and you have been to nearby cities, so you can probably make a fair guess at the landscape of that city. However, you may also been to some cities that were more built-up, more polluted, more hilly, so you maybe imagine the possibility of different types of landscape mixed in.

It is interesting to see what other forecasters have said about the perils of prediction. Sir Arthur C Clarke, well-known science fiction author (who also covered the Moon landings with Walter Cronkite, and is cited as the inventor of the geosynchronous satellite) liked to talk about the failure of nerve and failure of imagination. Failure of nerve relates to not really believing that something revolutionary may happen. Failure of imagination might be a smaller form of failure of nerve. There have been some very rapid changes in the economy and it seems to be getting faster so we need always to check back against a failure of nerve and imagination. Not forgetting of course that there may only be 5 years from the recession to the next boom.

In giving this talk many times, the closer I was to the last recession, the harder it has been to get people out of their funk and look optimistically into the future. In a recession and the slower recovery after, there is often a persistence of under-confidence, a pendulum swing from the overconfidence that occurs on a boom. It takes time for this feeling to dissipate which explains why there is no sudden return to massive growth levels of the previous boom. But, for those who can look ahead, it gives you time to get ready. Make sure you use it!

Lots of people use scenarios, by the way. When the Military do an exercise, they decide which side you are on, tell you where your forces are positioned, what has suddenly happened, what your objectives are and then let you get on with it. They then see what happens. If the other side manages to do an end-run around your electronic countermeasures or sneak in around the back, then those would be good reason to beef up in that area in real life. Or, after the so-called "flash crash" of the late 2000s when the stock market dipped 20% for 30 minutes and tripped many computerized stock market automated programs, now stock markets have regular exercises to see whether their newly-devised defenses are going to work. Some enterprises hire hackers to try to break their security.

The wilder the scenario the better, if you want to see what is really driving things.

So, in considering when the next boom may be, or what it is likely to be like, think different scenarios and different timings and see what difference that might make. If the boom comes 2 years earlier than expected, could you adapt? If it is delayed by 3 years, could you make the payments on your investment?

Some forecasters are interested in the difference between risk and uncertainty. Uncertainty is the probability of scenario A happening, say 30%. Risk is what is the likely impact of scenario A occurs, say $30 million. Professional forecasters combine risk and uncertainty into an "expected value", in this case 30% x $30m =$9m. That way you can try to compare which scenario is likely to affect you more. Rather clever. Except that you can spend a lot of time guessing and tweaking the figures. And we all have a tendency to alter the figures to get the result we secretly want.

I personally prefer the breakeven probability method of checking my assumptions., Maybe it will work for you, too. Let's guess you are a property developer. You think there's a 50% chance you sell it for a $2 million profit. But you are worried about not being able to sell the building for 2 years which might bring you a profit of $1m million say. (If you had to guess, you might estimate that the chances of not being able to sell the building for 2 years as 30%, say.) For the expected value of either outcome to be the same, then the outcome x the probability for event 1 must equal the outcome x probability of event 2. I.e. 50% x $2m=p% x $1m, where p=probability of event 2. So p%=(50% x$2m)/$1m=100%. But your best guess is that there is no way the chance of not being able to sell the building for 2 years as 30%, say.)

Samuel Brittan has pointed out[2] there is a difference between economic forecasts and scientific forecasts, which leads economic forecasts to be highly likely to be wrong. Scientific predictions are conditional. For example the temperature of water when it boils will be 212F or 100C, if the atmospheric pressure is the same at sea level and the pot is not enclosed. Economic forecasts are unconditional, that is, they take all that is current as a given, and make firm assumptions about the future in order to make a hard number in a forecast. This is what is likely to make it wrong. As a compromise, given the time periods involved between now and the next boom, we can make our best guess and list our assumptions, and then look at how sensitive the forecast is to those assumptions. Then we can run some scenarios with differing assumptions.

References and Further Reading

"This Time It Is Different: Eight Centuries of Financial Folly," Carmen Reinhart & Kenneth Rogoff

"Recession Storming: Thriving in Downturns through Superior Marketing, Pricing and Product Strategies," Rupert Hart

"SuperAbundance," Bain

"The Next Boom: What You Absolutely, Positively Have to Know About the World Between Now and 2025," Jack Plunkett.

"The Structure of Scientific Revolutions," Thomas Kuhn

"The Tipping Point," Malcolm Gladwell

"Innovation: The Attacker's Advantage," Richard N Foster

"CrowdFund Your Startup! Raising Venture Capital using new CrowdFunding Techniques," Rupert Hart.

"Animal Spirits"

Index

Notes

[1] Financial Times May 26 2011
[2] Financial Times May 26 2011

Made in the USA
Monee, IL
06 November 2026

68030314R00063